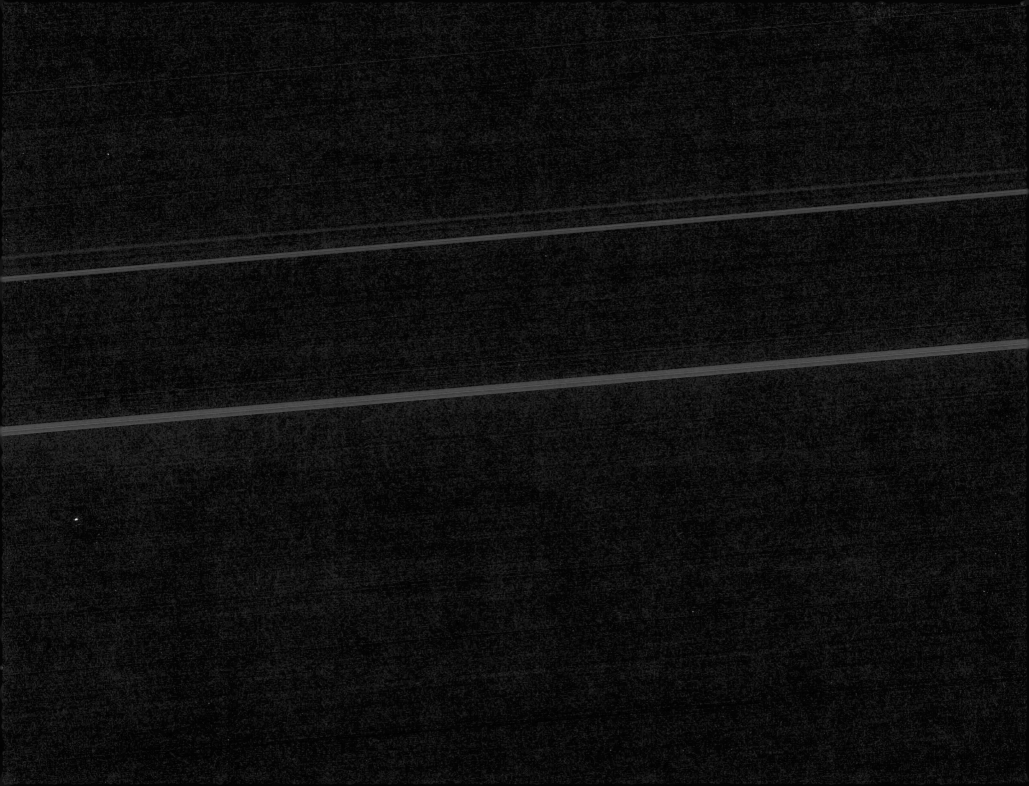

ELIM100
CENTENARY

Acknowledgements

In writing and compiling this book we have been conscious of the vastness of the task. This book cannot claim to be comprehensive or exhaustive. It seeks to give a popular and accessible account of the story of the Elim movement over the past 100 years and to show something of the vitality and vision of Elim today. Inevitably, we have found that there are many personalities, episodes and stories that we have not been able to include in this volume simply for lack of space. We have sought to tell the story in a way which centres on the "movement" of Elim through the significant seasons of its life so far and to shine a light on some of the many "defining moments" which have shaped the story.

The book draws on the extensive Elim Archive materials held at Elim International Centre, Malvern. We have also drawn on stories from local churches, first-hand accounts and testimonies and a wide range of publications to bring together a mosaic of words and pictures which we trust will capture something of the "evidence of the grace of God" over the 100 years of Elim. They are selective glimpses only – but we pray they will bless and inspire. We expect and hope that this book will stimulate individual Elim churches and ministries to mark their own Centenary in the coming years in creative and engaging ways.

This has been a team effort. As we have written, edited and compiled, we have been so thankful for the writing, ideas and photos submitted from a host of contributors. Special thanks to: Andy Wopshott, Andy Cogdon, Sharon Millar, Elim Historian Maldwyn Jones, Eric Gaudion, Archivist Phil and Sally Thomsett, Michael and Peggy Greenway, Edwin Michael, Gary Gibbs, Paul Hudson, Tim Alford, Dave Newton, David Butcher, Marilyn Glass, Alistair Cole, Mark Lyndon Jones, John Waller, Duncan Clark, Leanne Mallett, Bill Chapman, Bruce Atkinson, Michelle Bennett, Wayne Carpenter, Sarah Cogden, Tony Cauchi, Peter Wreford and the Direction Team, and the many churches which contributed photographs and materials. A huge appreciation to David and Jan Holdaway, who have taken an idea and made it a reality.

Chris Cartwright

Written, compiled and edited by:
Chris Cartwright
Jan and David Holdaway, www.lifepublications.org.uk

© Elim Pentecostal Church November 2014
www.elim.org.uk
Published by: Elim Pentecostal Church
ISBN 978-1-907929-65-6

Cover Design: Graeme Moodie
Internal Design: Graeme Moodie, Ruth Moodie, Kim Ballantyne, Anthony Harper and Shaun Burden   www.pwamm.com

For further information and downloadable resources on Elim History and the Elim Centenary visit www.Elim.org and www.ELIM100.org

DEFINING MOMENTS

100 YEARS OF THE ELIM PENTECOSTAL CHURCH

ELIM100
CENTENARY

Commendations

I send greetings on the occasion of the 100 year Anniversary of the moving of the Spirit that birthed the Elim movement.

We extend congratulations and thank God for all that He has done and the impact you have had around the world. We commend the many leaders who through the years have been faithful to the Foursquare Gospel we proclaim – of Jesus the Saviour, the Healer, the Baptiser in the Holy Spirit and the Coming King.

As we join you in celebration, we rejoice in what God has done and also rejoice in what He is going to do. May this be a celebration that is a springboard to the next era. Happy 100th!

Pastor Jack Hayford, Foursquare Church,

Chancellor and Founder, Kings University, Los Angeles and Dallas, USA

I want to bring my greetings on behalf of the fellowship of the Assemblies of God on this great occasion of your Centenary – one hundred years of witness and testimony in this nation. A testimony that has affected the world.

We are thrilled that the ongoing relationship between our two denominations is growing ever stronger. I believe in the power of synergy. Where God finds us dwelling together in unity, there He commands the blessing.

As our sister fellowship we say "Well done! Keep going for it! The best is yet to come!"

John Partington,

National Leader, Assemblies of God, Great Britain

The history of the world-wide church in the twentieth century is dominated by an amazing move of God with hundreds of millions coming to Christ, millions of churches planted and the emergence of a fresh, radical and passionate expression of the Christian faith. From humble beginnings 100 years ago, Elim as part of this Pentecostal movement, has profoundly influenced the church here in the UK.

I, and millions like me, have benefited from a fresh discovery of the work of the Holy Spirit, both in individual lives and in the body of Christ.

I'm thankful that Elim is not resting on its history but is looking forward to playing its part in the purposes of God in our generation.

Steve Clifford,

General Director, Evangelical Alliance

In my capacity as the National Leader, and on behalf of the National Leadership Team and members of the Apostolic Church worldwide, we join together with you to give thanks to God for what He has done in and through the Elim Pentecostal Church, in the United Kingdom and Ireland and in the many nations of the world.

A century of continuous, unbroken and growing witness to the gospel of our Lord Jesus Christ is a wonderful and significant milestone that is worth recognising and celebrating. To God be the glory for great things He has done. It is unquestionably His doing, and marvellous in our eyes.

Like Samuel of old, the Apostolic Church join you as you put down your corporate stones, in remembrance, commemoration and also thanksgiving to the Lord for the selfless service of those who have gone before us. We also join you in laying down stones prophetically, and by faith, to speak into the future, declaring that the light of the gospel would continue to shine even more brightly through Elim. We make bold to declare that this Centenary celebration shall be the catalyst and platform for the accelerated advancement of Christ's kingdom through the Movement; the beginning of a greater and better tomorrow.

Emmanuel Mbakwe,

National Leader, Apostolic Church, UK

Index

100

INTRODUCTION

Welcome to this very special publication marking one hundred years of our Movement's history.

Throughout the pages that follow you will read thrilling accounts of the early days as our Movement was brought to birth, extracts from defining moments in the years that followed and something of our vision, hopes and aspirations for the days that lie ahead.

In Elim we like to honour the past without living in it. That is why, while drawing from a treasure trove of precious memories, we have sought not to indulge in sepia-tinted nostalgia at the expense of recognising the challenge of a changing culture that God calls us as a Movement to minister into.

While God is the Ancient of Days He is also the God who 'makes all things new.'

Nor do we want to enshrine the traditions that brought us to where we are any more than a spacecraft wants to retain the empty fuel cells that propelled it into orbit which, unless jettisoned, become impeding ballast rather than a means of engaging in a new trajectory.

Traditions are potentially dispensable – only doctrines are eternal.

When God challenged Moses at the burning bush He introduced Himself as the God of Abraham, Isaac and Jacob – emphasising the long march of a faithful past. But He did not do so without presenting one of the greatest challenges ever given to a single individual – the proclamation of emancipation for millions who were being held in bondage.

If there is anything that we want you to embrace as you unpack with us the journey of the last century it is this:

God is with us in our history but He is every bit as present in our destiny.

John Glass

General Superintendent

Elim Pentecostal Church

SECTION 1

Honouring Our Past

Defining Moment

It's that moment…
when everything clicks

It's a 'yes' moment
It's a 'together' moment
It's an 'I was there' moment

It's that moment…
a soul is saved
a life is filled
a body is healed

It's a moment…
that defines a generation
that shapes a movement
that creates 'a people'

It's that moment…
when the past and the future collide with the present
when prophetic imagination is ignited
when a compelling vision is cast

It's a moment…
that propels fired-up disciples into mission
that moves followers further and faster
that compels believers to radical devotion

It's a moment…
that demands consecration
that calls for sacrifice
that requires face-down surrender

It's that moment…
when the wind blows
when the fire falls
when the earth shakes

It's a 'holy ground' moment
It's an 'immeasurably more' moment

It's that moment…
one space
one people
one God

Duncan Clark

*I will pour out
my Spirit
on all people...*

Joel 2:28

The Pentecostal Outpouring
A century of Pentecost

The early years of the twentieth century were marked by extraordinary outpourings of the Holy Spirit and a heightened sense of evangelism and mission.

The nineteenth century had ended with many Christians around the world crying out to God for a Christian revival. There was a renewed appetite for the scriptures with Bible camps and conventions. There were also calls to prayer and the beginnings of missionary movements which were starting to turn an introverted and largely comfortable church outwards to the nations. Yet growing numbers of believers became convinced that unless God was to empower the church with the Holy Spirit as at the dawn of the church in the book of Acts, they could not hope to reach the world for Christ. They needed and cried out for another Pentecost.

The beginnings were in a Bible School in Topeka, Kansas, USA, in the first days of 1901, when a handful of students were "baptised in the Holy Spirit" and spoke in tongues. They had been praying and earnestly seeking God in three hour shifts, 24 hours a day. God answered their prayers as they cried out to Him.

It was recounted:

"On the third of January, 1901, suddenly twelve students were filled with the Holy Ghost and began to speak with other tongues, and when Brother Parham returned and opened the door of the room where they were gathered, a wonderful sight met his eyes. The whole room was filled with a white sheen of light that could not be described, and twelve of the students were on their feet talking in different languages.

Apostolic Faith, October 1906

A new Pentecostal era had dawned.

Stone's Folly, Topeka, Kansas, was the home of the Bethel Bible School run by evangelist and preacher Charles Fox Parham from 1900 to July 1901. Parham, his wife Sarah and a group of about forty students and their families lived and worked in the unusual building which was built as a mansion in 1887 then abandoned due to an economic downturn. It was here that Parham instructed his students to examine the Bible, particularly Acts 2, to learn the biblical sign of Spirit baptism and on January 1, 1901, that Agnes Ozman, became the first student to speak in tongues.

Charles Parham   Agnes Ozman

Stone's Folly, Topeka, Kansas

The Welsh Revival – 1904 and 1905

Returning to his home in Loughor, Wales, from Bible College on Monday October 31, 1904, 26 year old Evan Roberts, a former coal miner who was training for the ministry, was convinced that God was about to send a mighty revival to Wales.

For years men and women in Wales had been praying for God to move once more in a land that had seen many revivals and moves of God over the centuries. At the end of the meeting that evening in Moriah Chapel, Evan asked permission for an after meeting with those willing to stay. For the next two hours Evan pleaded with the sixteen adults and one child who remained to confess Christ.

Over the next two weeks Evan Roberts led meetings in chapels throughout the area. More and more people stood to confess Christ until, in the second week, the Holy Spirit fell upon the meetings as people cried aloud for God to "send the Spirit for Christ's sake."

This Revival dawn at Loughor soon gave rise to a move of God throughout Wales which saw over 100,000 people converted. Evan and teams of young people as well as established ministers travelled all over Wales preaching, singing and sharing the Gospel. There were documented accounts of remarkable conversions and communities changed as the power of God impacted the church and culture of the day. The Revival in Wales gave hope and inspiration to people from across the globe who were trusting God for something similar in their own area. People came from far and wide to see and hear what was happening and news of the remarkable events in the Welsh Revival touched the world.

Evan Roberts

"The greatest known revival in church history.

Watchman Nee, Chinese writer and church leader, describing the Welsh Revival of 1904-05

Memorial to Evan Roberts at Moriah Chapel, Swansea

Azusa Street, Los Angeles

destroyed by fire. Its most recent use had been as a livery stable and its neighbours were a timber yard and a tombstone factory. However, church leaders and missionaries from around the world were drawn to the meetings at Azusa Street, which often went well into the next morning, as they sought the spiritual power with which they could take the gospel into a new century. From Topeka, Kansas, where on the first day of the new century, Agnes Ozman, was baptised in the Holy Spirit when her Bible School classmates laid hands upon her, to the Welsh Revival of 1904-1905 and then Azusa Street, Los Angeles, in 1906, the news and the experience of another Pentecost brought multiplied thousands into a fresh encounter with God.

*A*t Azusa Street, Los Angeles, California, a young black preacher William Seymour, a former student of Charles Parham, held open meetings where crowds flocked to seek and experience for themselves this new Pentecost.

Seymour, the one eyed son of former slaves, had been locked out of a local church building for preaching the doctrine of the baptism of the Holy Spirit when he first arrived in Los Angeles, but now found a spiritual home where he could minister. From 1906 the Azusa Street Mission became the launch pad for the fledgling Pentecostal movement as thousands were filled with the Holy Spirit.

It was an unusual setting to have such a great impact. The building, which one newspaper referred to as a "tumble down shack", was built initially as the home of the African Episcopal Methodist Church and had been partly

The Azusa Street Mission in Los Angeles, California, and the preaching of William Seymour became the launch pad for the fledgling Pentecostal Movement as thousands were filled with the Holy Spirit. At the time Los Angeles was a city of just over 100,000 people having grown from 5,000 inhabitants in the 1850s.

Azusa Street leaders

William Seymour and his wife Jenny

Azusa Street today

THE AZUSA STREET MISSION

The Azusa Street Revival was remarkable as in an era and place of racial segregation men and women, black, white and Hispanic all joined together in the move of God.

Pentecost comes to Britain

The vicar of All Saints Church, Monkwearmouth, near Sunderland, Rev Alexander Boddy had been sent by his church to Wales in 1904 where he met Evan Roberts. Hungry for a move of God in his own parish, the well-educated Boddy had stood in the Revival meetings in Wales and been humbled by the way God was moving in such ordinary surroundings.

Alexander Boddy   T.B.Barratt

Hearing of an outpouring of God's Spirit in Oslo, Norway, through the ministry of Englishman T.B.Barratt, the following year Boddy travelled to Norway to see what was happening first hand. He invited Barratt to Sunderland where, in late 1907, special meetings were held which led to around 19 people being baptised with the Holy Spirit and speaking in tongues. Among others these included a young Ghanaian who led a small group of believers in Peckham, South London, and a Bradford plumber by the name of Smith Wigglesworth.

Boddy's church became a centre for the renewed Pentecostal message and ministry as from 1908 onwards the Sunderland Conventions drew crowds of people from around the UK and the world to experience a fresh outpouring of the Holy Spirit.

His magazine *Confidence* took news of the new move of God around the world with many testimonies and reports of salvation, healing and pioneering mission and outreach.

Mary Boddy

Alexander Boddy's wife, Mary, was a descendent of John Wesley's wife, a widow named Mary Vazeille. In 1899 Mary Boddy experienced a healing from asthma and she and her husband both believed that she had a gift for healing through the laying-on of hands. It was Mary who laid hands on Smith Wigglesworth to experience the baptism in the Holy Spirit when he visited Sunderland in 1907. Smith Wigglesworth went on to have an outstanding worldwide ministry with many documented miraculous healings.

SEPTEMBER 1907.
WHEN
THE FIRE OF THE LORD
FELL
IT BURNED UP THE DEBT.

One of the results of the Pentecostal outpouring in Sunderland was that the debt on the church building was cleared.

Smith Wigglesworth

The Story of George Jeffreys
Beginnings

The Revival which swept Wales in 1904 and 1905 profoundly changed not only the church and chapel culture of the day but had a direct impact on the wider society. Stories of dramatic conversions and changed lives and communities travelled around the world. Within just six months of the outbreak of Revival in the small community of Loughor, near Swansea, on October 31, 1904, more than 100,000 decisions for Christ had been recorded in Wales.

Amongst those thousands were two brothers, Stephen and George Jeffreys from Maesteg in the Llynfi Valley, a few miles from Bridgend in South Wales. Stephen, a miner in the local pit, had been under conviction following the conversion of some of his co-workers. In Siloh chapel one Sunday in November he surrendered his life to Christ along with his 15-year-old younger brother George. Immediately, Stephen and George propelled themselves into the work of the chapel and growing in their new found faith.

While the Welsh Revival was drawing to a close, another movement was beginning thousands of miles away, centred on the Azusa Street Mission in Los Angeles, which would spread the news of a fresh Holy Spirit outpouring. Many ministers, Christian workers and missionaries began to receive the baptism in the Holy Spirit and soon the Pentecostal experience and what was becoming known as "the full gospel message" was being preached and proclaimed all over the world.

When the Pentecostal message and manifestations first came to their area George and Stephen had initially been sceptical. Yet, George and Stephen were themselves baptised in the Spirit in summer 1910 after Stephen's son Edward returned from holiday having "received a definite baptism of the Holy Spirit and begun to speak in other tongues as the Spirit gave...utterance."

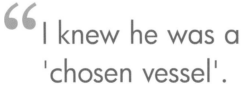

I knew he was a 'chosen vessel'.

Rev Glasnant Jones, minister of Siloh Chapel, who recognised the hand of God upon the brothers and took a special interest in George.

George Jeffreys as a child

" At the open air revival services I always found young Jeffreys at my side. I was privileged to give him his early religious tuition and a splendid scholar he was. Superior to other lads, there was a character in his face: I knew he was a 'chosen vessel'. When I left Siloh, Maesteg, in 1907 the young Jeffreys was in business, and had he remained in that calling, I am convinced he would have become a merchant prince.

Rev Glasnant Jones

Healing and Calling

Though his minister had seen something of the call of God upon his life, young George Jeffreys did not seem an obvious choice for the ministry.

He suffered from poor health and his general physical weakness was compounded by a severe stammer and a facial paralysis which pulled his muscles to one side. One Sunday morning while he was praying he received a complete and total healing. Healed and newly filled with the Holy Spirit, George began to set his heart on following his growing sense of the call of God.

George tells of his experiences in a letter in August 1910 to William Oliver Hutchinson, Bournemouth, pastor of the first church to be built and opened as a Pentecostal church in Britain.

Pastor William Hutchinson

Dear Pastor Hutchinson,

I really think that God would have me bear my testimony to the glorious work he has done in me. Hallelujah, since I have been at Bournemouth all things are become new, old things have passed away. I have been saved, sanctified, baptised in the Holy Ghost with the scriptural sign of tongues (Mark 16:17) and healed of sickness. This is the Lord's doing and it is marvellous in our eyes. Glory to God: God has taken the cigarette from between my lips and put a hallelujah there instead. Hallelujah. I have a gift of tongues and interpretation but the latter gift must still be developed. I cannot tell you all He has done for me as no tongue can glorify Him sufficiently. I feel free and happy, so very joyful, anxious to do something. Now comes my testing. I am going home to Wales and it is but the beginning of a mighty battle. But the Lion of the tribe of Judah does not tell me to fight alone but He Himself will do the worst part and victory is always His. I thank you for your prayers.

George Jeffreys

We were kneeling in prayer one Sunday morning…It was exactly nine o'clock when the power of God came upon me, and I received such an inflow of divine life that I can only liken the experience to being charged with electricity. It seemed as if my head were connected to a most powerful electric battery. My whole body from head to foot was quickened by the Spirit of God, and I was healed. From that day, I have never had the least symptoms of the old trouble. Many times since then I have relied upon the Spirit's quickening power for my body.

George Jeffreys

As told in the book
Healing Rays

Training

George's Pentecostal experience closed the door to the denominational colleges for theological training, yet, with the encouragement of Cecil Polhill he applied in September 1912 to the Council of the Pentecostal Missionary Union (PMU). They recommended he go to their Bible School in Preston led by Thomas Myerscough. He began his studies in November, his fees paid by the wealthy Polhill.

The PMU Bible School became a magnet to young men eager to take the gospel to the nations in the power of the Holy Spirit. George's classmates included William F.P. Burton, the pioneer missionary to the Congo who would pastor the Elim Mission at Lytham prior to setting sail for Africa. Here he met Ernest Darragh from Bangor, County Down, who would become his closest friend for almost 40 years and Ernest John Phillips from Bedford who would work alongside him in forming and developing the Elim Movement.

The students who enrolled at the PMU Bible School had set their sights on overseas missionary work. They were heading for the nations. Yet, whilst George was there he received a clear sense of God's call to the United Kingdom which to some would be a dramatic departure from the purpose and focus of his training. For George personally and for evangelism in the United Kingdom however, it was to be a defining moment.

> " From England, Ireland, Scotland and Wales, young men came to sit at the feet of Thomas Myerscough…It is doubtful whether any school has ever achieved so much in view of the short time that they were in Bible School.
>
> Desmond Cartwright

Thomas Myerscough and Pentecostal Missionary Union students

George Jeffreys' first ordination certificate

The First Miracle

After just a short time in Bible School, George left to help his brother Stephen and George was "set apart for the ministry by the Independent Apostolic Church known as Emmanuel Christ Church, Maesteg, on November 13, 1912."

Stephen had seen a breakthrough in a series of meetings which he was conducting in Cwmtwrch near Swansea, Wales. Many had come to faith in Christ and Stephen had preached for weeks without a break. He was desperate for help and sent for George. In seven weeks they saw 145 converts. Following this, urgent invitations flooded in for the brothers to hold meetings in other places.

At Penybont, near Llandrindod Wells in January, 1913, Edith Carr who had been lame with a diseased foot, was completely healed after the brothers anointed her with oil and prayed with her. It was the first outstanding miracle of the Jeffreys brothers' ministries and the news brought increased crowds to their meetings.

It was the first of a string of remarkable healings that would form a vital part of almost every mission they conducted over the next twenty years. Whilst the brothers did not believe that the healings brought salvation in themselves to those healed, they did recognize them as the Lord confirming His Word *"with signs following"* and as attracting people to hear the gospel.

> " A great light came round me, and filled me with great power, and I arose from the couch and stood on both feet, and walked gently round the room with scarcely any help.
>
> Edith Carr, healed in 1913

Sunderland

In response to their growing reputation George and Stephen were invited by Alexander Boddy to speak at his Sunderland Convention of 1913.

George went with a group from Wales and his ministry made a strong impression. His preaching, in particular, made a real impact on a young Irishman, William Gillespie from Belfast. Gillespie and his brother, also called George, soon invited Jeffreys to Ireland to hold meetings, boldly sending him three ten shilling notes for the boat fare. George's decision to go to Ireland would be momentous and see the birth of a new Pentecostal movement, within a decade churches were opening all over the United Kingdom.

The Gillespie brothers, William and George, who invited George Jeffreys to Ireland and sent the money for his boat fare.

George Jeffreys, standing second from left, with the leaders of the Sunderland Convention 1913.

Sunderland International Pentecostal Convention 1913

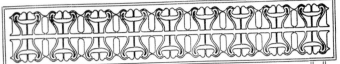

THE LONDON CONVENTION. Page 111.

JULY, 1916.
VOL. IX. NO. 7.

"CONFIDENCE"

EDITED BY

ALEX. A. BODDY,

ALL SAINTS' VICARAGE, SUNDERLAND, ENGLAND.

PICTURE-VISION OF CHRIST.

The X marks the place on the wall where it appeared in Island Place Mission, Llanelly, So. Wales. (Bro. Stephen Jeffreys in the Rostrum.) Page 113.

"This is the CONFIDENCE that we have in Him, that if we ask anything according to His will, He heareth us: And if we know that He hear us, whatsoever we ask, we know that we have the petitions that we desired from Him."—1 *John* v., 14-15.

100th ISSUE.

ONE PENNY.

London : Samuel E. Roberts, Publisher, Zion House, 5a, Paternoster Row, E.C.

Miraculous signs

Stephen Jeffreys had taken on the pastorate of Island Place Mission, Llanelli, in 1914. On Sunday July 5, Stephen was preaching on the text "that I might know Him, and the power of His resurrection, and the fellowship of His suffering," Philippians 3:10.

Jeffreys said that he was conscious of a tremendous anointing and extra power and blessing as he was preaching, and he could see the people were riveted in his direction. On the wall behind him as he preached there appeared a remarkable picture. First it was blurred and indistinct but soon it became clear that it was the face of a lamb. After some time it changed to the appearance of Christ as the Man of Sorrows. The vision remained on the wall for around six hours where it was seen by hundreds of people. The building was finally locked at 2am the vision still there but by next morning it had disappeared.

The local newspapers reported the incident interviewing many who had seen the vision. The vision was thoroughly investigated and many accepted it as a sign from God. The vicar of Well, near Litchfield, Rev J.W.Adams, twice visited Llanelli in 1926 and then the following year. He questioned many eye witnesses and listed scores of people who could confirm the story. The most detailed account recorded is in *Confidence*, the magazine edited by Rev Alexander Boddy of Sunderland, which was printed in July 1916.

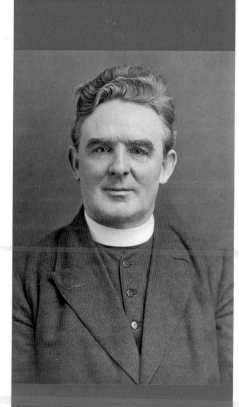

" We remained in the chapel for a long time looking and scores of others who heard about it came to examine. Among them was a strong skeptic, who declared, 'I have seen and now I believe.' He came in an infidel and went out a believer.

Stephen Jeffreys

CERTIFIED COPY of
COPI DILYS O

an ENTRY OF BIRTH
GOFNOD GENEDIGAETH

Pursuant to the Births and

Deaths Registration Act 1953

| Registration District | | | | | | | | |
| Dosbarth Cofrestru | | | Bridgend | | | | | |

1889

BIRTH in the Sub-district of
GENEDIGAETH yn Is-ddosbarth

Maesteg

in the
yn

County of Glamorgan

Columns:— Colofnau:—	1	2	3	4	5	6	7	8	9	10*
No. Rhif	When and where born Pryd a lle y ganwyd	Name, if any Enw os oes un	Sex Rhyw	Name, and surname of father Enw a chyfenw'r tad	Name, surname, and maiden surname of mother Enw, cyfenw a chyfenw morwynol y fam	Occupation of father Gwaith y tad	Signature, description, and residence of informant Llofnod, disgrifiad a chyfeiriad yr hysbysydd	When registered Pryd y cofrestrwyd	Signature of registrar Llofnod y cofrestrydd	Name entered after registration Enw a gofnodwyd wedi'r cofrestru
	Twenty eighth February 1889 24 Metcalfe Street Maesteg U.S.D.	George	Boy	Thomas JEFFREYS	Keziah JEFFREYS formerly BROWN	Collier	Keziah Jeffreys mother 24 Metcalfe Street Maesteg	Sixteenth April 1889	William David Registrar	—

Siloh Chapel, Maesteg, where George and Stephen became Christians.

George was born on February 28, 1899, in 24 Metcalfe Street, Maesteg. His mother was Keziah Brown before she married, and his father Thomas was a collier.

OGWR in the yn

COUNTY OF MID-GLAMORGAN

for the above-named Sub-district, and that such Register is now legally in my custody. yr Is-ddosbarth a enwyd uchod, ac a gedwir yn gyfreithlon gennyf i.

P. J. Zillo

Superintendent Registrar
Cofrestrydd Arolygol

Cofrestrydd

anrhyw berson (1) sy'n achosi rhoi manylion anghywir ar y dystysgrif hon neu (2) sy'n defnyddio ...rif anghywir fel un gywir, ac yntau'n gwybod ei bod yn anghywir, yn agored i'w erl...

> "From the first of the meetings God has been saving souls, and sinners have been trembling under conviction of sin. One young man was stricken down from his seat by the power of God and was saved and immediately delivered from sin.
>
> George Jeffreys

ELIM EVANGELISTIC BAND

The Beginnings of Elim
Monaghan

George was initially invited to hold meetings in Monaghan, Ireland, where a group of young men were fervently praying for God to move in their community. The Methodist Hall they had booked was refused them and the first mission cancelled after it was discovered they were Pentecostals.

For a season George continued his itinerant ministry holding meetings across the UK until, at the end of 1914, he returned to Ireland. After preaching at a convention in Belfast the same young men who had initially invited him to Monaghan, and who had been meeting for prayer in an upper room in the town, asked to meet with him again.

On Thursday January 7, 1915, in Knox's Temperance Hotel, Monaghan, George met with six young men: Albert Kerr, George Allen, Frederick Farlow, Robert and John Mercer and William Henderson. They came together as the minute book of the Elim Evangelistic Band would record "for the purpose of discussing the best means of reaching Ireland with the full Gospel on Pentecostal Lines."

They determined that,

"George Jeffreys, of South Wales...be invited to take up a permanent evangelistic work in Ireland and that a centre be chosen by him for the purpose of establishing a church out of which evangelists would be sent into towns and villages, and that a tent be hired, for the purposes of holding a Gospel Mission during the month of July to commence the work in Ireland."

At their second meeting in July two workers, Ernest Darragh and Margaret Straight, joined the Evangelistic Band. Darragh had studied at the Pentecostal Missionary Union (PMU) Bible School but Margaret Straight had been rejected as being "too fanatical." A tent mission was planned for George Jeffreys and the team in North Road, Monaghan. It was clear that the hand of God was upon the work.

The Elim Movement had begun.

The tent at Bangor which attracted visitors from Los Angeles, New York and London.

The tent in Monaghan, 1915

The First Elim Church

In August 1915 William Gillespie and Ernest Darragh sought a place in Belfast which could serve as a centre for the ministry. They found a disused laundry in Hunter Street and rented it on a three year lease as a Mission. George began meetings and was installed as pastor of the first Elim church which was given the name "Elim Christ Church".

They began winning souls and establishing not simply one but a number of congregations. George produced a booklet, *What We Believe*, outlining the doctrines of the new church making it clear that they believed they were "contending for the faith" in contrast to the modernism and liberalism of others. They agreed to this first statement of faith and that "no member of any other assembly be asked to join the church."

By October 1917 their building was proving hopelessly inadequate for the crowds and they bought a disused church in Melbourne Street. This was Elim's second church. The new movement was set on a course of expansion which would see it grow to twenty one workers and fifteen churches in Ireland by 1920.

One of the striking features of these pioneering days was the growing number of outstanding men and women who joined the ranks of Elim and became prominent in the emerging movement. These included former Preston student E.J.Phillips, John Carter from Birmingham (later the General Superintendent of the Assemblies of God), E.W.Hare, former president of the Cambridge University Christian Union and Cyril Taylor, a final year medical student who became one of Elim's first missionaries, ordained in April 1920 for service in the Belgian Congo, (pictured above).

Hunter Street, Belfast: The first Elim church pictured in 1932

" It was clear that they had no intention of establishing a new denomination. It was their desire to be an evangelistic agency with the express purpose of reaching out into a needy district where they sought to win people to Christ.

Desmond Cartwright, *The Great Evangelists*

Why Elim - What's in a Name?

In Wales many chapels were given individual names, usually drawn from significant places in the Bible. There were chapels all over Wales with names like Horeb, Ebenezer, Bethel, Moriah (which featured in the opening days of the 1904 Revival) and Salem. One such name was Elim.

The name occurs in Exodus 15:27, *"Then they came to Elim, where there were twelve springs and seventy palm trees..."* It was a place of refreshing on the journey of the Children of Israel from the bondage of Egypt towards the land of promise.

Lytham in Lancashire where George Jeffreys first came across the name Elim

George had also come across it as the name of the Pentecostal Mission in Lytham, Lancashire. He had preached there a number of times whilst a student at the nearby PMU Bible School. He had commented to the mission's founder, Thomas Mogridge, that if he built a church he would call it Elim. It seems likely that he had intended to call the next "Ebenezer" but the name Elim proved popular and was soon associated with the new movement and so they kept it.

The members of the new Evangelistic Band lived "on faith lines." They shared any money or gifts and trusted God for their every need. Times were tough as Britain was engaged in fighting a war on the continent of Europe. Their evangelistic zeal was matched by a courage and sacrifice which saw them ready to pay any price to reach men and women for Christ.

Then suddenly, and unexpectedly, news was received that George had been made the chief beneficiary of a sizeable estate left to him by a lady who had died in North Wales in 1917. The will was contested however, and a barrister friend, John Leech K.C., advised him to register his Evangelistic Band under the name of the Elim Pentecostal Alliance. This legal registration gave the group official recognition as a denomination and would also save George from tax on the legacy. They did not receive the legacy until 1925 and the greatly reduced sum of £1,000 was used to pay off the debt on one of the church buildings in Ireland.

The Elim church had begun officially and plans for its development were growing daily.

Donald Gee

George Jeffreys has been described as possibly the most gifted and influential preacher the British Pentecostal Movement has ever produced. Donald Gee, a Pentecostal statesman of the early years, gives a revealing account of him,

" He had a voice like music, with sufficient Welsh intonation to add an inimitable charm. His platform personality at times was magnetic. His face was appealing. Although lacking academic training he possessed a natural refinement that made him acceptable in all circles. He presented his message with a logical appeal and a note of authority that was compelling. With all that he was baptised in the Holy Spirit.

from Tent

to Tabernacle

The country town of Monaghan in Ireland was the birthplace of Elim. John Wesley is reputed to have preached the Gospel in the town, for which he was imprisoned for one night. Here, under canvas roof, the first Elim Revival Campaign was held.

George Jeffreys says of those first meetings,

"Monaghan is a place situated almost in the heart of Ireland, where John Wesley was imprisoned for preaching the same Gospel which I am now privileged to proclaim. Although many years have passed…the gospel… is still proving itself to be just as powerful in the convicting and saving of precious souls these days in the very same town. From the first of the meetings God has been saving souls, and sinners have been trembling under conviction of sin. One young man was stricken down from his seat by the power of God and was saved and immediately delivered from sin.

By October 1917 the Revival group's first building in Hunter Street was proving hopelessly inadequate for the crowds who were coming to the meetings. A disused church in Melbourne Street was bought to meet the growing needs. It was a taste of the expansion that was to follow in the coming years to meet the demands of the number of people finding salvation and healing through the Pentecostal message.

An Early Testimony

Adelaide Henderson was at one of the very early Elim meetings in 1915. Fifty years later she wrote her testimony of the encounter that changed her life.

'On a cold December afternoon, Boxing Day, 1915, we were sitting together at my home having tea with Miss Boyle, our missionary friend from India.

From behind the teapot came mother's voice. "Where would you like to go to church tonight, Miss Boyle?"

"To hear a young evangelist in a Mission Hall in the city," came the reply. "You will go too," said mother, looking at me.

My heart sank! Mission Hall of all places. Too hot a place for my guilty conscience. Too much of a challenge to my way of life, which was far from keeping step with my godly home.

Into the less residential part of Belfast with its cobblestone streets we went, and presently found Hunter Street and the much dreaded Mission Hall. Brilliantly lighted and packed to the door, this one-time laundry struck terror to my heart as Miss Boyle and I pushed our way right to the front to get seats. Led by a fair young man with a breezy winning smile, they were raising the room with *Rescue the Perishing*. On and on they sang beating time with their hymn books, as Mr Darragh led them from the platform with his irresistible charm. How I wished myself safely back in the staid security of Old Park Presbyterian Church where I had been a worshipper with my family.

But now the dark-haired Welsh man took over. It was Mr Jeffreys and how he preached! I sat shivering, conscience stricken.

"Hypocrite, hypocrite," cried my conscience. "Get out of this before that tornado of burning eloquence finishes you off."

I struggled towards the door with a bumping heart and stiffened as a firm hand was laid on my shoulder. I had missed my chance!

"Where are you going?" It was my brother's voice. "I can't stand this another moment. Let me go! This place is too hot for me," I cried.

But Willie did not let me go. Kneeling by his side and under great conviction of sin, I accepted Christ as my Saviour. Was ever a brother more pleased and was ever a sister more relieved and happy as we made our way home together.

Ten days later I received the baptism of the Holy Spirit. Friends, this baptism is a sacred and blessed experience. It so revolutionised my life that after fifty years I can truly say the fires are still burning. How people can attend a Pentecostal Church and enjoy the vibrating life-giving power of the meetings and not seek eagerly to receive the baptism of the Spirit, is something (I believe this solemnly) for which they will have to give account before Almighty God.'

Adelaide Henderson

was a school teacher in 1915. It was World War I and she also became a policewoman as part of her wartime duties working four hours a day after school hours using the opportunity to witness to soldiers and civilians. She went on to become one of Elim's first missionaries, going to the Congo in 1922 but later returned due to ill health. She was a tireless supporter of missions and had a powerful prayer ministry. She died aged 91.

Dowlais, in South Wales, was the first Elim church on mainland Britain and Stephen Jeffreys its first pastor. Behind him on the wall crutches and a boot can be seen on display, left behind by those healed. The church also had a Spanish speaking congregation drawn from the iron and coal workers living nearby who had been reached by the new Pentecostal message.

Expansion: The Word Spreads

*T*he infant Elim movement, and George Jeffrey's ministry in particular, was gaining the attention of many in mainland Britain. This was helped significantly by the small Elim group publishing their own magazine, The Elim Evangel, in December 1919. At "threepence" a copy, it provided a "record of spiritual life and work."

Initially, it was a quarterly publication with 2,000 copies printed in Tamworth by F.B.Phillips and carried personally to Belfast by his brother E.J.Phillips. Within two years the *Elim Evangel* became a monthly publication carrying reports of the growing numbers of pioneer campaigns as well as teaching and testimonies. In later years it became a weekly magazine.

The first edition of the *Evangel* showed the small group of evangelists and workers, led by George Jeffreys, growing in confidence, believing they were part of a fresh move of God. The cover contained a sketch of palm trees and wells and the text from Exodus 15:27, *"And they came to Elim..."*

Wales and the Channel Islands

By 1921 Pentecostal assemblies in the Welsh towns of Dowlais and Llanelli along with Guernsey (Vazon) on the Channel Islands had joined the Elim Pentecostal Alliance.

New converts being baptised at the Vazon Church in the Channel Islands

England

The first Elim church in England was at Leigh-on-Sea, Essex. A Pentecostal group had come together under the leadership of George Kingston, a local business man. George Jeffreys went to conduct eight days of meetings, first in a drawing room, then in a newly built Mission Hall. In October 1921 George Kingston was ordained as the pastor and the church joined Elim. Kingston remained in business while pastoring the new church and pioneering a group of churches in Essex. He was an early example of apostolic ministry as he worked tirelessly giving finance, leadership and tremendous energy to establish the churches as part of the growing Elim movement.

In the north of England, a former Salvation Army officer, Ernest C.W. Boulton, had been leading a small work in May Street, Hull. George Jeffreys was invited to hold meetings and many were added to the church. E.C.W. Boulton joined the Elim workers along with the Hull church. A gifted writer and musician as well as a pastor, he went on to hold many different leadership roles in Elim and wrote the first biography of George Jeffreys, *A Ministry of the Miraculous*. Written in 1928 the book tells of the ministry George exercised in towns and cities across Britain and contains many testimonies and photographs of people miraculously healed.

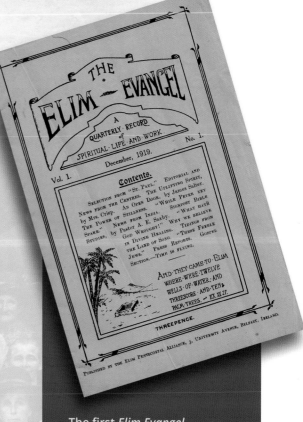

The first *Elim Evangel* December 1919

George Kingston

The Work in Ireland Expands

In Ireland the work progressed with vigour. A new hall was purpose built at Ballymena where Robert Mercer became pastor. Missions were conducted in Moneyslane, Portadown, Bangor, Eskylane, Cullybacky and Milford and a hall was rented at Armagh.

George Jeffreys laboured to establish the work of Elim in Ireland developing a strong bond with the young men who had invited him. He pitched the Elim tent at Lurgan but it was soon far too small for the crowds. The meetings moved to the Town Hall where despite 1,000 seats the meetings were still overflowing. Over 200 converts were recorded and the new church took up the task of discipling these Pentecostal converts with great urgency and dedication. George's methods were emerging from the intensity and drama of these "crusade" meetings. It was clear that the converts would not easily find a welcome in churches closed to the new Pentecostal message. They had no option but to form Elim churches, so George typically began a new church after the initial meetings with two weeks of nightly Bible instruction and then he appointed one of the Elim Evangelistic Band as pastor, to "shepherd" the new flock.

This continued to be his method as he moved into England, Scotland and Wales. As the numbers grew in the early 1920s however, it was clear that providing pastors would be a significant challenge and though they had seen around twenty churches planted in a decade, reaching a whole nation would take a level of spiritual breakthrough way beyond what they had so far seen. These early years were to be preparation for what was to come.

The Elim Evangelistic Band in Ireland

Ernest Darragh and George Jeffreys, Belfast, 1914.

A Dramatic Breakthrough

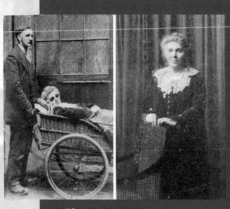

Mrs Altoft in 1914

In 1922 after her healing

A dramatic breakthrough was to come, in the words of a later Elim Evangelist, George Canty, "not in fervent Wales or evangelical Ulster, **but astonishingly, amongst some of the toughest workers and non-church going types in the land, at Grimsby."**

On January 7, 1922, Stephen Jeffreys held a small meeting at a home in the east coast fishing town of Grimsby. Alec Douglas, who was bent double with pain from an intestinal condition, was totally healed as Stephen and the small group at the meeting laid hands on him. Only a few others joined the meeting the next day at a local auction room. Stephen was discouraged and said he was going home. The now healed Alec Douglas said, "No you are not! God sent you and you are staying." Word began to get around the town of healings at these meetings and soon no hall was big enough to contain the crowds. Hundreds were converted with reports of "fishermen going to sea rejoicing in their new found saviour". Elim songs were heard everywhere with the old electric trams running along the seafront full of passengers singing the songs from the Elim meetings.

There had literally been an explosion of healings in the meetings with deafness, arthritis, ruptures, tumours and heart conditions vanishing. One war wounded man who had lost bone and muscle tissue from his arm and shoulder and had been unable to move it was seen swinging his arm above his shoulder.

Healings

A Mrs Altoft, who had been ill for eleven years and could only get about using a spinal carriage, was healed while lying in the carriage during one service. She said she suddenly felt as if "mighty hands were lifting her up to heaven". For some time her carriage lay on the piano in the new church with a sign declaring, "She is not here, she is risen!"

Stephen preached and ministered non-stop for 12 weeks until he was exhausted. George came to take the meetings forward with the change of style and personality in no way diminishing the manifestations of God's power. The crowds increased and they moved to the 3,000 seat Skating Rink. The numbers grew to 5,000 and when the meetings finally ended crowds gathered to bid the Jeffreys brothers farewell.

The Grimsby mission had demonstrated that God was confirming His word with signs, wonders and miracles and this would be both the expectation and pattern for the Elim movement over the next few years. Though the Jeffreys brothers had remarkable gifts and God was using them to spearhead a fresh move of His Spirit, it was evident that the same Spirit was resting upon ordinary believers who would take Him at His word.

There were numerous accounts of healings, many of which were verified by the medical profession. This testimony of a doctor, printed in the local paper, illustrates the powerful impact that physical healings were having in drawing many to the Elim meetings:

180, Kennington Park Road,
S.E 11.
April 15, 1921.

I hereby certify that Edith May Cufiley has been under my professional care since December, 1917, and before that date, under my predecessor, the late Dr Foster Owen, for several years. She was rendered unfit for work in June, 1916, by reason of pulmonary tuberculosis, which was followed by spinal tuberculosis. She was more or less prostrated from that time until the 4th of April last, when she appears to have mysteriously recovered, having received no systematic treatment since her removal from a sanatorium in August, 1920. For the last two years she was crippled, bed-ridden, and believed to be incurable. In my opinion, she is now recovered and will soon be quite fit for work, and her cure can only be ascribed to her wonderful faith in prayer.

(Signed) P. EUGENE GIUSEPPE, M B., C M., J.P., Late Government Medical Officer, Trinidad, B.W.I.

Clapham

While the power of Pentecost was falling in Grimsby, the Elim leaders were also making plans to move their administrative base to London and, in the winter of 1922, they purchased a former Methodist Church in Park Crescent, Clapham. The building became the location of the first Elim church in London and the offices were transferred there, the site would also house the Elim Publishing Company.

Elim's departmental heads, George Jeffreys seated centre

The newly renovated Clapham Elim Church became the epicentre of Elim's growing identity as a Pentecostal Movement. George and his team lived in rooms behind the church hall. Stephen left Wales and joined his brother in pastoring the new church, which was later known as Clapham Central Church, as it was the headquarters of the movement. For five years the brothers pastored here and also conducted services throughout in the UK. Everywhere they went miraculous healings followed their preaching.

Here the first students received their training for ministry. Here they began to plan their outreach to the capital. Here they opened the Elim Bible College as a response to the need for training of ministers and workers. From here the Pentecostal message was sent out to other parts of the world as, in March 1922, Adelaide Henderson said farewell from Elim Tabernacle, Clapham, to serve in the Congo, becoming one of Elim's first missionaries. Soon other young pioneers were sent out from Clapham to spread the gospel in many parts of the world.

Clapham also became a centre for revival services with the Evangelistic Band and their followers holding regular

meetings where many people were converted, baptised in the Holy Spirit and healed. Events at Clapham, along with the subsequent healings, were widely reported in the press and verified by the medical profession.

Over the next five years Stephen and George held campaigns across England and Wales and churches were established in Letchworth, Plymouth, Ashbourne, Barking, Forest Hill, East Ham, and other areas of London. And they would soon head north to Scotland.

FOURSQUARE CRUSADERS

In the autumn of 1924, James McWhirter and the young people of Elim Clapham organized themselves into a youth ministry under the name Elim Crusaders. From the outset these Crusaders were encouraged into serving alongside the members of the Elim Evangelistic Band.

THE ELIM FOURSQUARE CRUSADER

JESUS

SAVIOUR
HEALER
BAPTISER
COMING KING

GOD'S BEST
FOR US
OUR BEST
FOR GOD

ELIM CRUSADER

Elim Crusaders, Swindon

The zeal and energy of the new young Crusaders was quickly felt as Crusader branches were opened in every church. Soon some were complaining that Elim was "entirely a youth movement." The leaders of the day answered: "There is room for both youth and age, zeal plus experience, grit as well as grace, the young recruit as well as the staid warrior in the ranks of the Lord's work."

Elim Bible College

The year 1925 ended with the purchase of another building in Clapham which had formerly been used as a convent. Woodlands became the home for the new Elim Bible College and an immediate answer to the increasing demand for men and women to be trained as pioneers, evangelists, missionaries, pastors and teachers. The students' class which had been started months earlier in the minor hall of the Clapham church gave way to a Pentecostal Bible College which drew a stream of men and women from Elim churches throughout the nation to train for ministry. Many of them arrived with very little materially, but they left with faith to change towns, cities and nations.

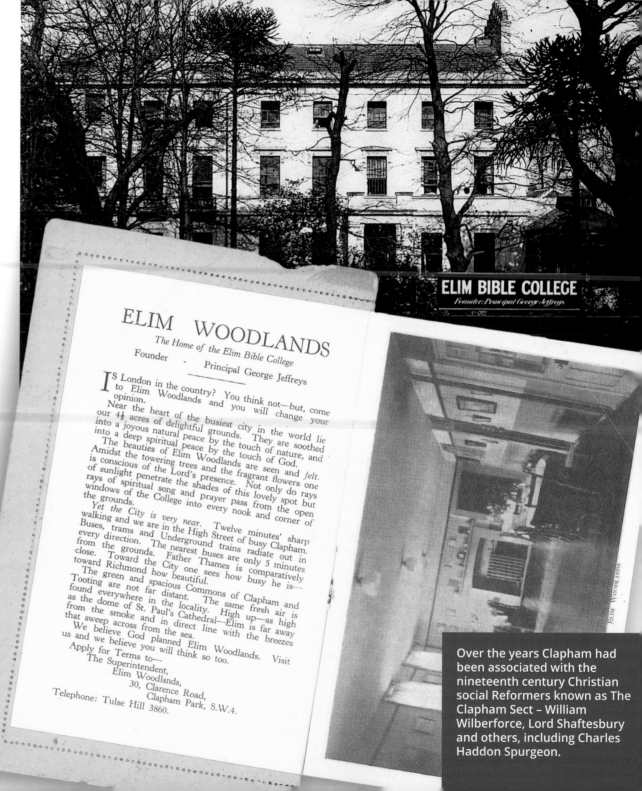

ELIM WOODLANDS
The Home of the Elim Bible College
Founder - Principal George Jeffreys

IS London in the country? You think not—but, come to Elim Woodlands and you will change your opinion.

Near the heart of the busiest city in the world lie our 4½ acres of delightful grounds. They are soothed into a joyous natural peace by the touch of nature, and into a deep spiritual peace by the touch of God.

The beauties of Elim Woodlands are seen and *felt*. Amidst the towering trees and the fragrant flowers one is conscious of the Lord's presence. Not only do rays of sunlight penetrate the shades of this lovely spot but rays of spiritual song and prayer pass from the open windows of the College into every nook and corner of the grounds.

Yet the City is very near. Twelve minutes' sharp walking and we are in the High Street of busy Clapham. Buses, trams and Underground trains radiate out in every direction. The nearest buses are only 5 minutes from the grounds. Father Thames is comparatively close. Toward the City one sees how busy he is—toward Richmond how beautiful.

The green and spacious Commons of Clapham and Tooting are not far distant. The same fresh air is found everywhere in the locality. High up—as high as the dome of St. Paul's Cathedral—Elim is far away from the smoke and in direct line with the breezes that sweep across from the sea.

We believe God planned Elim Woodlands. Visit us and we believe you will think so too.

Apply for Terms to—
The Superintendent,
Elim Woodlands,
30, Clarence Road,
Clapham Park, S.W.4.
Telephone: Tulse Hill 3860.

ELIM BIBLE COLLEGE
Founder: Principal George Jeffreys

Over the years Clapham had been associated with the nineteenth century Christian social Reformers known as The Clapham Sect – William Wilberforce, Lord Shaftesbury and others, including Charles Haddon Spurgeon.

MINISTERS OF THE ELIM FOURSQUARE GOSPEL ALLIANCE.

E. C. BOULTON.

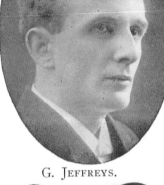

G. JEFFREYS.

J. T. BRADLEY.

W. M. BARTON.

H.

M. F. BARBOUR.

P. N. CORRY.

H. A. COURT.

D. BOULTON.

MINISTERS OF THE ELIM FOURSQUARE GOSPEL ALLIANCE.

W. HENDERSON.   G. KINGSTON   A. HENDERSON.   M. STREIGHT.

STRONGE.

A. COURT.   KELLY.

MINISTERS OF THE ELIM FOURSQUARE GOSPEL ALLIANCE.

FIELDING.

MINISTERS OF THE ELIM FOURSQUARE GOSPEL ALLIANCE.

R. A. MERCER.   J. MULLAN.   J. J. MORGAN.   J. McWHIRTER.

J. McAVOY.   J. R. MOORE.   W. A. NOLAN.   C. NOLAN.

J. NAYLOR.   S. A. PINCHBECK.   H. C. PHILLIPS.   E. J. PHILLIPS.

PHILLIPS.   L. C. QUEST.   J. C. REUSS.

In 1928 there were 97 ministers in Elim – 32 of them women. A number of these female ministers were married to ministers, others were evangelists and missionaries such as Dollie Phillips and Adelaide Henderson, who were among the first missionaries Elim sent overseas.

Timeline 1920-1930

PIONEER MISSIONS, SPECIAL MEETINGS
AND MINISTRIES

1920 Dowlais, Llanelli

1921 Leigh-on-Sea, Vazon in Guernsey join Elim, Stephen Jeffreys at Horbury Chapel, Kensington

1922 Grimsby, Hull, Clapham

1923 Letchworth, Tamworth, Ashbourne, Elim Leaders' tour of Scandinavia

1924 Elim Publishing Office built at Clapham, Elim Leaders' tour to North America

1925 Liverpool, Barking, Forest Hill, East Ham, Ilford, Elim Bible College opens, Surrey Tabernacle meetings

1926 Plymouth, Chelmsford, Bournemouth, Aimee Semple McPherson visit, Royal Albert Hall meetings begin

1927 Rochester, Carlisle, Glasgow, Paisley, Leeds, Brighton, Southampton, Wimbledon, Portsmouth

1928 Exeter, Eastbourne, Bradford, Hammersmith, King's Cross, Croydon, Reading, 1,000 baptised at the Royal Albert Hall

1929 Worthing, Ipswich, Greenock, Brixton, Cardiff, Swansea

1930 Birmingham, Wandsworth, Kingston upon Thames, Ealing, Crystal Palace meetings begin

Capturing The Cities
A surge of expansion

The period 1926 to 1930 saw a great surge of expansion for the Elim movement. In 1926 Stephen Jeffreys parted company from his brother, George, and left Elim to work independently. For George, these years saw God use him to fill the largest halls in Britain and become the most successful British evangelist since the days of Wesley and Whitefield. It was the time of the Great Depression and the General Strike of 1926, but this didn't deter people from flocking to the halls and churches to hear the Pentecostal message.

Of the many city wide and town campaigns which George Jeffreys and his campaign team conducted a number stand out, with thousands of converts, outstanding miracles of healing and strong new churches established which would become centres of Pentecostal ministry and mission.

The Revival Party

With the increasing demands of schedule, George Jeffreys put together a small but gifted team to help with the organisation and the public ministry of the pioneering missions. By 1929, the team was Ernest Darragh, James McWhirter and Albert Edsor. Darragh was the anointed and charismatic song leader, McWhirter the organiser who planned the campaigns, and Edsor, the young and gifted pianist (and regular chauffeur), who saw first-hand the meetings and the

miracles and, like a young John Mark in the gospels, wrote gripping eye witness accounts.

The five years from 1926 to 1930 saw George Jeffreys and the Revival Party blaze a trail of evangelistic campaigns throughout the UK. Typically, a hall would be hired, meetings would begin with small numbers, and word would spread as people responded. In many places a sudden and dramatic physical healing or miracle would result in crowds pouring into the meetings. George and his team would stay on, often hurriedly hiring additional halls, expecting and believing for God to move in even greater power. The following illustrations are drawn from numerous others which testify to cities being profoundly affected by the pioneering ministry.

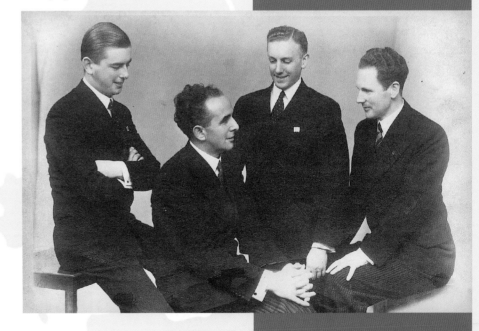

The Revival Party
Ernest Darragh, George Jeffrys, James McWhirter and Albert Edsor

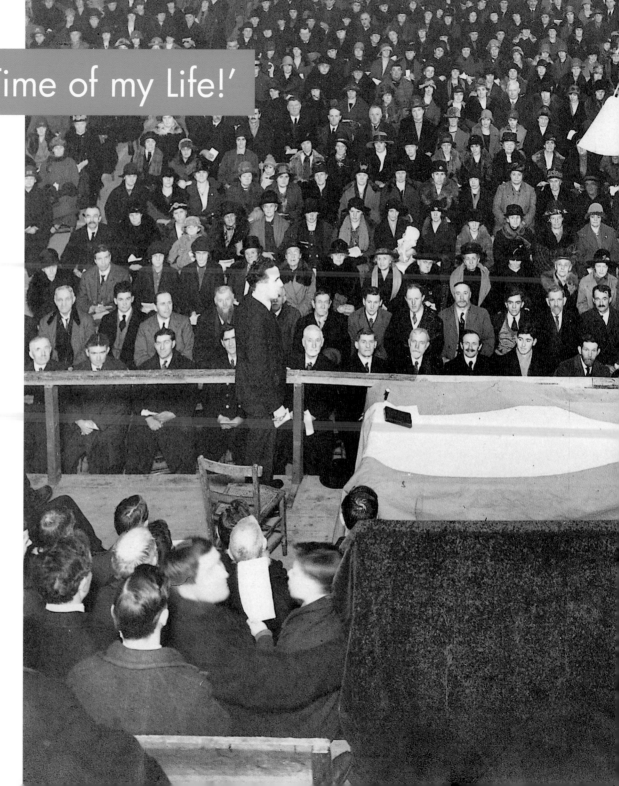

Plymouth 1926 – 'The Time of my Life!'

Beginning in January 1926 the meetings in Plymouth quickly drew thousands and George Jeffreys postponed other missions as he saw what God was doing. The only building which could accommodate the growing crowds was the huge Military Drill Hall, seating 6,000.

The success of the Plymouth meetings focused public attention on George himself. This was something with which he was never comfortable. Yet, he was conscious of the effect of the publicity in giving an audience for the gospel to be preached.

" I am having the time of my life. Souls are continually flocking to Christ, most startling and marvellous healings, while yesterday hundreds were turned away from the town hall an hour before starting time.
An average of about forty souls a day are being saved. Three who were crippled walked in the service last night. The ambulance brought one and arrangements had been made for it to come for her. However, she walked home. This is the greatest healing service yet.

George Jeffreys speaking about the Plymouth mission

Liverpool –
The Boxing Ring

Meetings in Liverpool, which had been postponed for the Plymouth meetings, eventually started on March 14, 1926. Hiring the vast Boxing Stadium in Lime Street, the local paper headline announced "Jeffreys in Ring Again!"

Heading North — Carlisle

At the close of 1926 George arrived in Carlisle at the invitation of a small group of Pentecostal people. Within a week there were dozens of converts and they looked for another hall.

The Military Riding School was a huge barn-like structure with no heating or seating. This did not deter the crowds who brought their own seats. Here, over the next few months, George and his team saw an amazing breakthrough, particularly amongst young people.

One of those young people was James T. Bradley. He entered the Elim ministry the following year and spent more than 45 years in a wide range of national roles including Dean of the Bible College, Editor of the *Elim Evangel* and Secretary General.

> There are hundreds of young people captivated the like of which I have never witnessed before. The salvation of souls is marvellous in every meeting, I cannot keep count…The cream of the city is now clamouring to get in…The healings are more and greater than anywhere. Today the place was stirred by a young lad whose arm was in splints and broken. After he was prayed for, his mother took off the splints and the arm was perfect. I cannot possibly tell you how we have gripped the city.
>
> George Jeffreys, speaking about his visit to Carlisle.

The mission made a huge impact upon the young people of Carlisle and by 1936 a thriving Crusader group was part of the church.

Leeds

George Jeffreys had visited Leeds twice before, but beginning meetings on March 20, 1927, this visit saw a major spiritual breakthrough. The meetings only lasted a short time but within two weeks 2,290 had professed conversion.

The Leeds church was totally inadequate to accommodate the crowds and they were forced to find larger premises for the church had been impacted by a "Day of Pentecost" scale outpouring of God's Spirit.

Again, major healings spread like wild fire across the city. James Gregson had been seriously injured in an industrial accident. His legs had been twisted and crushed to the point that he had to drag himself around on crutches. Reading an account of the meetings in the local paper and of a woman healed of blindness, James's wife encouraged her husband to go to the meetings. George laid hands on him and prayed. He was instantly healed. The change was so profound that within weeks he had put on over 30 pounds in weight, was the picture of health and was able to return to work as an iron maker.

James Gregson

James Gregson was a totally changed man after he was brought to George Jeffreys' Revival Campaign meeting in Leeds in 1927. For more than five years he had suffered intense agony due to a serious injury.

At the meeting he was unable to sit and had to be laid on the floor before the rostrum from which Jeffreys preached. He testified to his healing the next year before ten thousand people at the Royal Albert Hall meeting in Easter 1928.

Giving his testimony, he said,

> " When Principal George Jeffreys laid hands on me, the power of God came into my body and I was lifted from the earth and was instantaneously healed.

Before . . .

. . . and after his miraclulous healing.

Glasgow – Breakthrough in Scotland

***O**n January 23, 1927, meetings began in St Mungo Hall. On the first Sunday, 600 came by train from the new church in Carlisle to support the Glasgow meetings.* On arriving, they stopped traffic as they marched through the streets to the venue. Within a short time there were 150 decisions for Christ; by the end of the first month this had risen to 700. When the meetings closed at the end of March the number of converts exceeded 1,500.

As well as new converts, a significant number of experienced ministers and workers of great spiritual maturity and vision were drawn to the movement. Among these were W.G.Hathaway, who was leading a small group of independent Pentecostal fellowships in Glasgow, and Percy G. Parker, a former Congregational minister from Birmingham. Both joined Elim and were soon redeployed to the Head Offices in Clapham to sow their gifts and ministries into the rapidly growing movement.

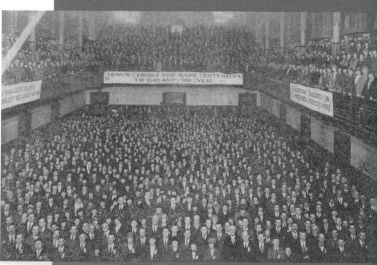

Glasgow

Dundee

Edinburgh

Dundee

Southampton – Miracles in the South

Meetings began with small numbers on April 21, 1927. The first night saw just four converts but numbers grew rapidly and the final days saw crowds filling the meetings with 120 decisions for Christ on the final night. An outstanding feature of the Southampton meetings was the number of remarkable healings, including that of Florence Munday who was totally healed of tuberculosis of the knee, a condition which had rendered her unable to walk and a Mrs Cox who was dramatically healed, no longer needing her wheelchair. A number of those healed went on to live long and active lives in Christian ministry.

Among those touched by the meetings was James Goreham from Romsey. He became a pastor and pioneer evangelist and was instrumental in the opening of five Elim churches in the late 1920s including Romsey, Salisbury and Andover. He died on July 5, 1934, aged just 25, from tuberculosis, however the churches he planted were thriving testimonies to his evangelistic work.

Pastor James Goreman: He planted five churches in his teens and early twenties before dying aged 25 from tuberculosis.

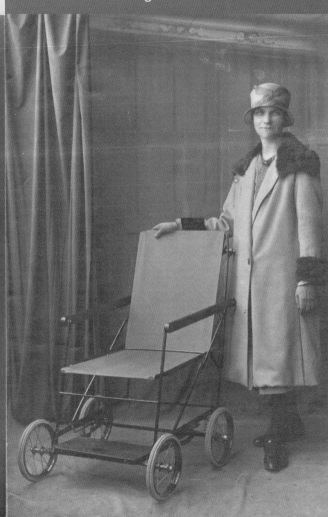

Cardiff 1929

In 1928 an anonymous postcard arrived at Clapham saying simply "Cardiff needs Foursquare Gospel!" On September 22, 1929, George Jeffreys and the Revival Team began meetings in the Cory Hall in the city centre. A handful of people were present in the first meetings and George wrote to E.J.Phillips, "It will take time..." After three weeks they counted 500 converts. Over 51 days more than 3,000 accepted Christ. It was the most successful campaign George and his team had seen to date. Cardiff was so impacted that as well as a church of 1,000 birthed out of the meetings, countless numbers of fired up, Spirit empowered believers flowed back into the surrounding Valleys with fresh faith for a new move of God in their communities.

Rev Glyn Thomas, in later years

Swansea

During the Cardiff meetings, some believers from Swansea asked George Jeffreys to consider coming to their city. The night after the Cardiff meetings closed, George began preaching in the Central Hall. It was November 11, 1929. He had not been to the city in almost 20 years, yet, despite being largely unknown and appalling weather, crowds came to hear.

It was here that the same reporter from the *Daily Express* who had recounted Evan Roberts' meetings in the Welsh Revival of 1904-5 described the Elim meetings and interviewed George. Again, outstanding miracles accompanied the preaching.

Glyn Thomas, a young hunchbacked man who sold newspapers near Swansea Castle and was well known locally, was amazingly healed. After prayer, the jacket he was wearing hung limply on his back and the huge hump completely disappeared. He was also healed of severe epilepsy. He went to study for the ministry pastoring churches abroad and throughout the UK.

One night, George's former minister, Glasnant Jones, now elderly and living a few miles away, came to the meeting to hear George. Within three months, Wales had seen a mighty move of God in the largest two cities with over 5,000 converts.

FAINTING WOMEN ON THEATRE STAGE.

Fervour at Evangelist's Meeting.

SWANSEA FLOCKS TO REVIVAL SERVICE.

Crowds queuing in Cardiff, 1929

> "...before any human hands were laid on me I felt two hands, which could have been none other than the hands of my blessed Saviour, placed upon my back, and there before that great crowd, that which the doctors had failed to do for twenty years, the Lord Jesus Christ did with one touch. The hump instantly disappeared and my bones were placed into their right position. The coat which I was wearing hung in folds upon my back. At the same time God delivered me from epileptic fits.

Rev Glyn Thomas, speaking later of his healing.

In the midst of these meetings a reporter from The Western Mail newspaper, who had interviewed Evan Roberts during the Welsh Revival of 1904-1905, compared what he saw in the meetings with the extraordinary events and impact of the earlier Revival.

Writing to E.J.Phillips as Christmas approached and with meetings scheduled for Belfast over the New Year, George knew he had seen a breakthrough in Wales. Greatly challenged that the reporter had seen this as similar to those Revival days, Jeffreys sought Phillips' wisdom on what he should do. It was as if, after witnessing more than 5,000 come to Christ in just three months, he had seen the nation of Wales opening up spiritually and ripe for a fresh revival.

He made the decision to go on with his scheduled meetings in Belfast and to honour the commitments he had already made for 1930. George returned to Wales only occasionally after this and never for any prolonged campaign. Yet, 1930 was his most fruitful and powerful year of ministry with tens of thousands accepting Christ most notably in Birmingham where the whole city was impacted.

Birmingham 1930

The meetings George Jeffreys held in Birmingham, beginning on March 26, 1930, were the greatest and most successful of his ministry. Meetings were due to close on April 13 but the number of converts was already into thousands and the sheer crowds meant even the Town Hall was too small.

Moving to the 8,000 seater Ice Rink, meetings throughout May were filled to overflowing. In June they hired The Bingley Hall, an exhibition hall which could seat 15,000 people. They filled it 26 times (a total of over 250,000 attended) and the final service began half an hour early since they could not fit anyone else in. In total, over 10,000 people accepted Christ as Saviour and George and his team baptised 1,100 before leaving the city. The announcement that they would open Elim churches in Birmingham following the crusade brought the Bingley Hall crowds to their feet. Three thousand turned out for the opening of the Graham Street Church, now Birmingham Christian Centre (BCC), and soon churches were opened in Oldbury Road and Sparkbrook.

" Imagine Bingley Hall crammed with seats and every seat occupied. Imagine the galleries crowded and people wedged tight in doors left open to let in the air...

The Birmingham Gazette

REPORTS

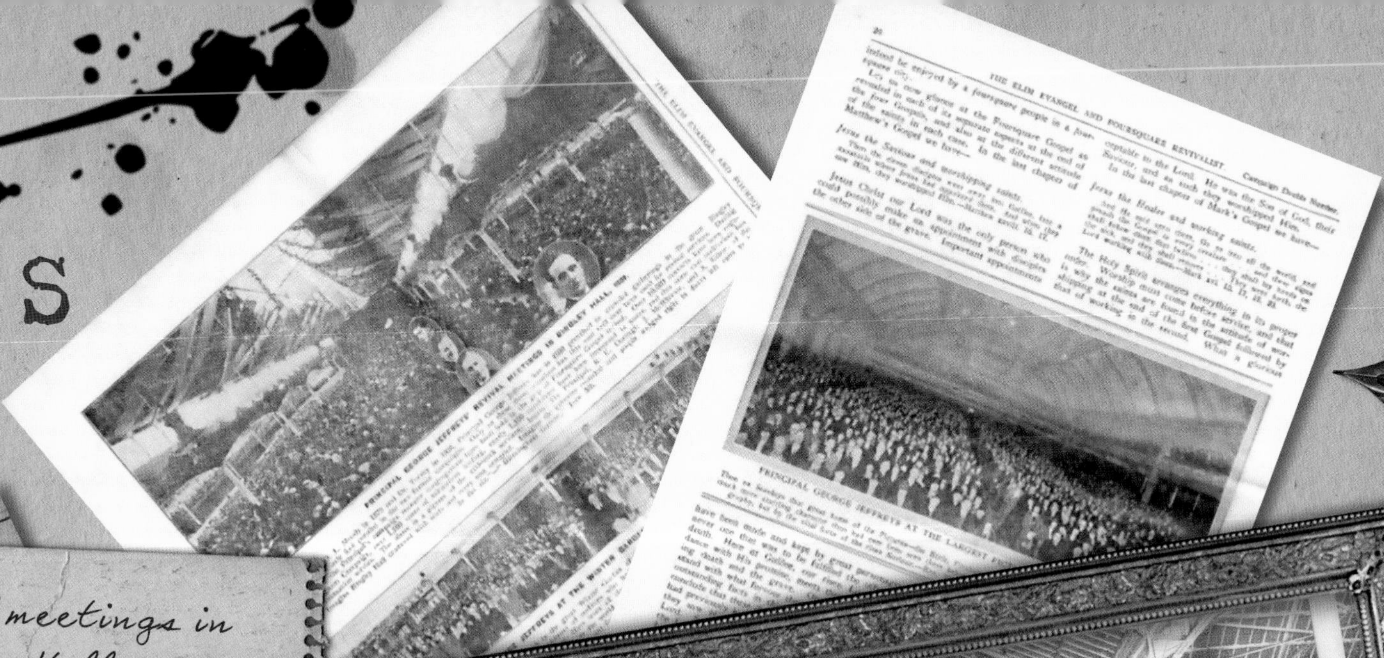

Reports of meetings in the Bingley Hall, Birmingham, 1930 and the Winter Gardens, Devonshire Park, Eastbourne, late 1928 in the Elim Evangel

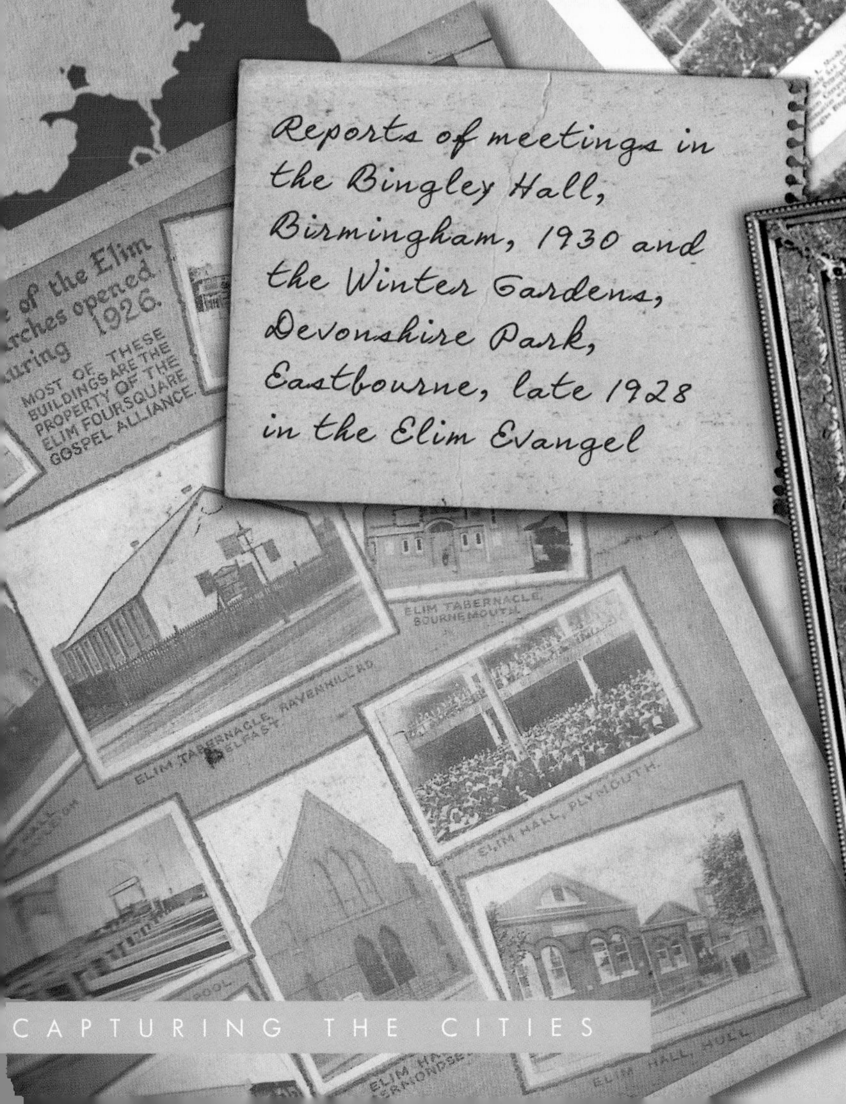

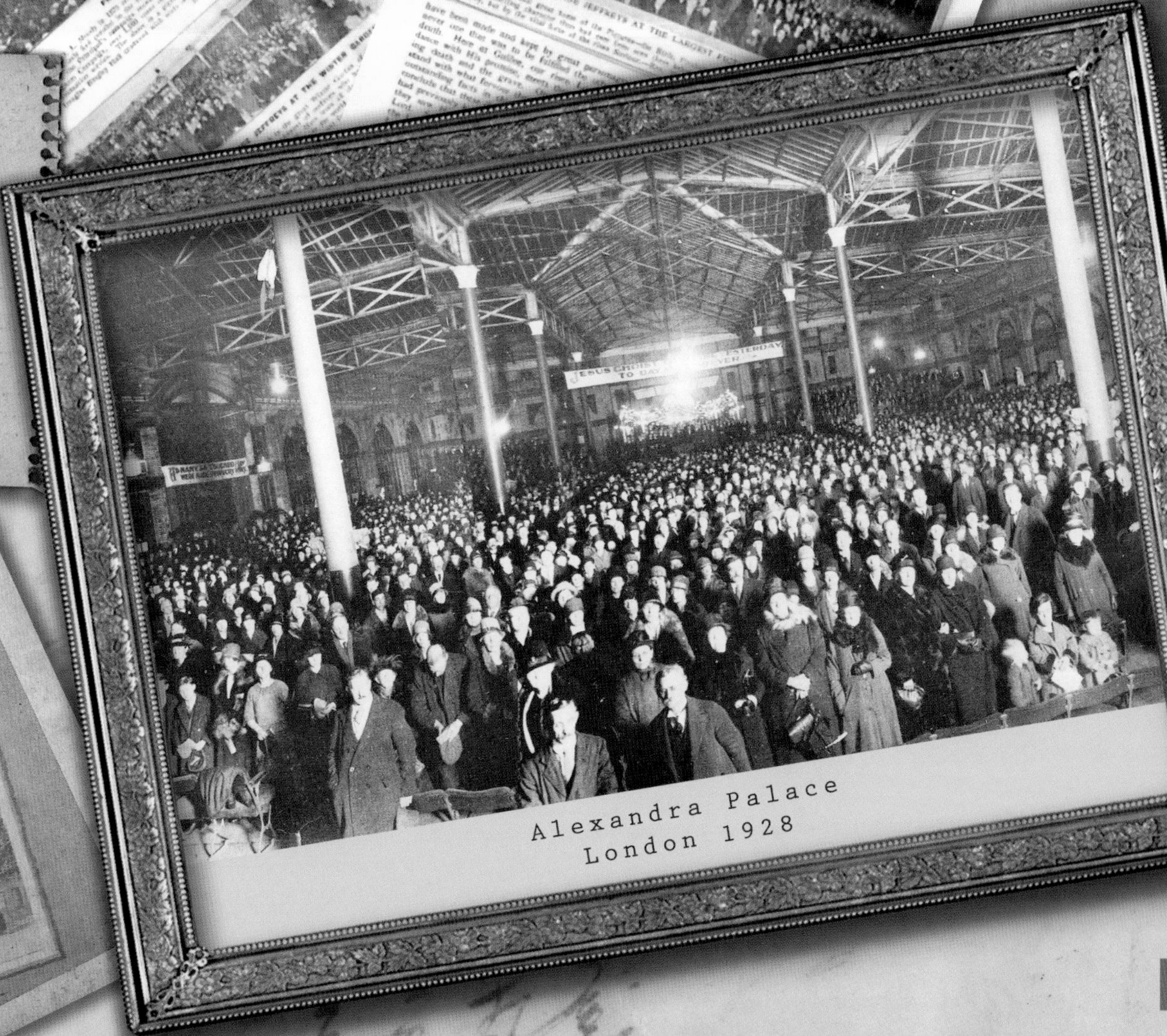

Alexandra Palace
London 1928

Advertising f...
meetings w...
everywhe...
such as in th...
barber shop ...
Canning Tow...
Londo...

Healings and Miracles

One of the most outstanding features of the campaigns and missions that took place were the number of healings and miracles that hundreds of people experienced. Wherever the Revival team went there were documented accounts of people being healed of sickness, paralysis and illness. Age and background were no hindrance to the power of God touching and changing people's lives as all over the country the healing power of God moved.

Helen Ewart, healed at the meetings in Edinburgh.

Agnes Radcliffe, healed of paralysis at Birmingham.

H.S.M. Smith. Healed of a growth at the Crystal Palace.

Joseph Mackie, healed at Glasgow after being crippled through septic poisoning.

Mrs M.McWilliams was healed at Ulster Hall, Belfast, of epileptic fits.

Miss Basford. Her right eye was healed at a campaign in Scunthorpe.

Nora Gutteridge, healed of a rupture at the Royal Albert Hall, Easter Monday, 1933.

The healing of Florence Munday was one of the most amazing miracles seen during the Revival campaigns. She had been crippled with tuberculosis and bedridden with ailments for about fourteen years when she was healed at the meetings in Southampton in May, 1927. She was the first of the 1,000 people to be baptised in the Royal Albert Hall the following year on Easter Monday.

Miss Levick, helpless hand restored at Birmingham Campaign.

Jessie Robertson. Healed of an ulcerated stomach at a campaign in Perth.

A gathering of those healed at the celebration and Revival meetings in Belfast.

The Miraculous Healing of Miss Florence Munday

THE first time I saw Miss Florence Munday was at Easter, 1928, across the length of the Royal Albert Hall, when she appeared among the 1,000 candidates that were immersed by Principal George Jeffreys at the great Elim baptismal service on that occasion—the first to step into the waters of burial with Christ. And as I had heard her marvellous experience quoted by others, albeit in fragments, I was glad to win from the lips of herself and her mother the story of our Lord's healing power and grace, when the two ladies visited the Elim Bible College.

Miss Munday looked very little more than half her years, a circumstance which made me remark that when the Lord healed her, He must have made her over again. She impressed me as a natural, normal and open-hearted young woman, to all appearance still in her early twenties; and certainly nothing in

Elim at the
Royal Albert Hall

Meetings at the Surrey Tabernacle in the mid-1920s were so successful they began to focus George Jeffrey's mind on the impact of conventions as a vehicle for "demonstration" of Pentecostal ministry and experience. Yet a seemingly small request set him looking to a bigger stage – the Royal Albert Hall – and to initiating a huge annual Pentecostal event which became a defining feature of the Elim movement for decades.

An Unexpected Call

In February 1926, George received an unexpected call from the American evangelist Aimee Semple McPherson who wanted to hold meetings in London the following week on her way to France. George and the Elim team invited her to speak at the Surrey Tabernacle convention and hurried through publicity. All 2000 seats were filled and powerful meetings saw many baptised in the Holy Spirit and healed. She planned to return for Easter.

When the press heard of Aimee's visit, there was huge interest. At the time she was the most famous woman in America with her huge Angelus Temple church in Los Angeles attracting vast crowds from down and outs to Hollywood stars. Jeffreys and the Elim leaders decided they needed a bigger venue and quickly booked the Royal Albert Hall for Easter weekend. Aimee preached on Sunday night and Easter Monday. The press gave extensive coverage and the event was a great success. Even though Aimee's flamboyant style was not to everyone's taste, Elim had made a move to the Royal Albert Hall and the following years saw extraordinary demonstrations of God's saving power in the most famous hall in the nation.

Elim Foursquare

After the tragic death of her husband, Robert Semple, while the newlyweds were serving as missionaries to China, Aimee Semple MacPherson set out as an itinerant evangelist preaching all over America. She settled in Los Angeles and made such an impact that in 1923 she opened the 5,000 seat Angelus Temple. It was then the largest church in the world. George Jeffreys and his group visited Angelus Temple on a tour of America in 1924 and they were introduced to Aimee.

Aimee had called her churches Foursquare and George Jeffreys found the name appealing. Upon his return he began to use and popularise the term and it began to be used to summarise the essential priorities of the Pentecostal message: Jesus the Saviour, Healer, Baptiser and Coming King. It provided a popular focus for preaching and soon Elim people were being called "Foursquare Gospellers" and attracting even more attention.

George Jeffreys felt that the word Foursquare should be included in Elim's title. After much discussion, in 1929 the Elim Foursquare Gospel Alliance (EFGA) became the official title of the Elim Movement. In time the Foursquare term was dropped for all but administrative purposes and the older name of "Elim" and Elim Pentecostal Church more commonly used.

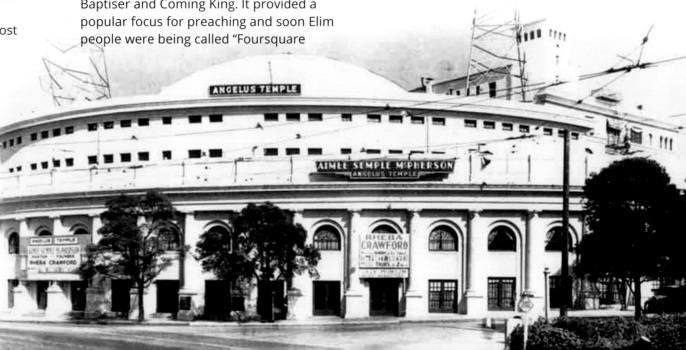

Angelus Temple, Los Angeles

Aimee Semple McPherson

ter that year, on Thursday May 20, 1926,
eorge Jeffreys received a cable from Aimee
mple McPherson's mother. It read:

ISTER MCPHERSON DROWNED WHILE
WIMMING TUESDAY... WHOLE WORLD
OOKING TO ANGELUS TEMPLE
OURSQUARE.

VANGELIST IMPERATIVE. NEED YOU HERE
MEDIATELY THIS CRISIS HOUR.

ABLE EARLIEST POSSIBLE DATE YOU CAN
AVE" - Mother Kennedy

eorge had just begun the city to city
mpaigning which saw many healed and tens
thousands of people come to Christ. Here was
desperate plea for him to lead Angelus
mple, the most famous church in the world.
eorge and Elim prayed and eventually he
sponded that the work of Elim in the UK
eant that he could not come. Soon Aimee
appeared claiming she had been kidnapped
d a storm of controversy surrounded her
inistry for years to come.

eorge Jeffreys and the Elim movement went on
a decade of some of the most fruitful
angelism that the towns and cities of Britain
ve ever seen.

1,000 People Baptised

*T*hough Elim would make the 10,000 seat Royal Albert Hall
*their Easter home for many years, 1928 saw a high point
when, on Good Friday morning, more than 1,000 converts
were baptised in a one ton portable tank measuring eight by
six feet and four feet deep.*

The doors of the Royal Albert Hall had to be altered to get
the tank inside. E.J.Phillips' masterly planning brought
together a large team of workers and young ministers to
assist George Jeffreys in one of the largest baptisms in
church history.

While the Royal Albert Hall Easter meetings were a focal
point, Albert Edsor, a member of Jeffrey's Revival Party
reporting in 1937, noted that the packed Royal Albert Hall
was only one of fifteen Elim "Foursquare Gospel
Conventions" being held that day in different parts of
England, Ireland, Scotland and Wales.

" Over a thousand people passed
through the waters of baptism, and as
Principal Jeffreys immersed them, songs
of praise, choruses that thrilled the
heart, rang up to the mighty dome.
Next morning, almost every newspaper
in the land contained reports and
photographs of that remarkable service.

Bible College principal Percy Corry describing the
baptismal service in 1928.

George Jeffreys baptising in the Royal Albert
Hall, 1928.

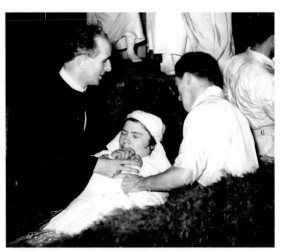

Baptising in the Royal Albert Hall, 1939.

The Royal Albert Hall with baptismal candidates seated.

DEFINING MOMENTS

ROYAL ALBERT HALL

MANAGER — CHARLES B. COCHRAN

FOURSQUARE GOSPEL DEMONSTRATION

EASTER, 1931
Easter Monday, 11 a.m., 3 p.m., and 6-30 p.m.

SPEAKER: PRINCIPAL GEORGE JEFFREYS

ADMIT BEARER

EASTER MONDAY (3 meetings)

Doors open one hour before each meeting
Special Singing by Elim Crusaders for ½ hour before each meeting

PRESS

ENTER BY ARTISTS' ENTRANCE

THIS TICKET TO BE RETAINED AND SHOWN ON DEMAND

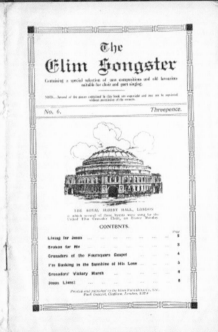

Jesus Lives!

Crusader Choir Piece No. 40.

ELIM CHORUSES, No. 1
A Collection of 52 Choruses, words and music. Now in its 7th edition

ELIM CHORUSES, No. 2
Another 55 different Choruses, including many favourites. 2nd edition

ELIM CHORUSES, No. 3
Another 66 different Choruses, including many favourites. 2nd edition

ELIM CHORUSES, No. 4
Our latest selection of new Choruses, words and music

The above chorus books are obtainable at 6d. each (by post 7d.), or all four books post free for 2/-.

ELIM PUBLISHING CO., LTD., PARK CRESCENT, CLAPHAM PARK, LONDON, S.W.4.

The Elim Songster

Containing a special selection of new compositions and old favourites suitable for choir and part singing.

NOTE.—Several of the pieces contained in this book are copyright and may not be reprinted without permission of the owners.

No. 6. Threepence.

THE ROYAL ALBERT HALL, LONDON
at which several of these hymns were sung by the United Elim Crusader Choir, on Easter Monday

CONTENTS

	Page
Living for Jesus	2
Broken for Me	3
Crusaders of the Foursquare Gospel	4
I'm Basking in the Sunshine of His Love	5
Crusaders' Victory March	6
Jesus Lives!	8

Printed and published by the Elim Publishing Co., Ltd., Park Crescent, Clapham Park, London, S.W.4.

---

100 Baptised By Preacher In Big Tank

By a Special Correspondent

A REVIVALIST preacher achieved yesterday an ambition which the most famous impresarios of our time have failed even to approach.

He is Principal George Jeffreys, leader of the Four Square Gospel Alliance.

At his annual revivalist rally he filled the Albert Hall three times in a day—filled it so that people were standing and kneeling in galleries, boxes and around the arena.

At each service there were fully ten thousand enthusiastic followers of his creed.

In the morning, he announced, miracles of healing were performed. Among those who pronounced themselves cured were:

20 cripples;
72 cases of cancer, tumour, or other growth;
17 cases of blindness in one or both eyes;
18 people who were deaf;
70 people suffering from rheumatism and stiff limbs.

Principal Jeffreys

At night over 100 men, women and children dressed in white were baptised by total immersion in a large tank erected below the platform.

One by one they were "ducked" by Mr. Jeffreys and an assistant, in the blue glare of powerful searchlights, while the congregation sang rousing hymns and shouted "Hallelujah."

It was announced that 131 converts had been made at the meeting.

Amazing Faith Cures Claimed

SPOTLIGHTS PLAY ON 'FOUR SQUARE' BAPTISMS

THREE times ten thousand people assembled in the Albert Hall yesterday. Ten thousand came in the morning, ten thousand in the afternoon, and ten thousand at night.

They came to hear Principal George Jeffreys of the Elim Four Square Gospel Alliance. They came to testify their faith in salvation through Jesus Christ. They testified in words, in song, and in prayer.

It was not the old and the feeble who came. It was the youth of Britain. Three-quarters of the vast congregations were between the ages of eighteen and thirty-five.

From among them came those who had been sorely afflicted. They came forward to the platform in the limelight to testify to the faith which had made them whole.

Of those who testified seventy-two acknowledged cures from cancer and malignant growths; twenty had been cripples; seventeen had been blind; seventy had been afflicted with stiff muscles or useless limbs; eighteen had been deaf.

ROAR OF "HALLELUJAH"

"A time of tribulation has come upon the earth," Principal Jeffreys declared with flashing eyes. "I would say 'Get back to the Bible, get back to God.' This great Empire would not have to trouble about the future if she would bow the knee to God."

Then as he expounded his Gospel he broke off to say: "I believe there are thousands here who would give a great shout of salvation. Say 'Hallelujah!'"

A roar of a great salvo of guns filled the hall.

Then the baptism began. Spot-lights shone on the tank of water before the platform. A microphone was placed in position.

Six sturdy young men in white flannels stood in the tank with Mr. Jeffreys. One by one the candidates were baptised. First a husband and wife, then some men, then women.

There were white-haired converts and children barely in their teens. They came in seemingly endless procession until more than 100 had been baptised.

Baptising at the Royal Albert Hall.

Candidates robed and ready to go into the baptismal waters.

Nottingham Elim Members ready for the train to the Royal Albert Hall, April 1933.

The 21st Anniversary celebrations at the
Crystal Palace, London. Crowds of
12,000 attended the meetings.

Coming of Age
1931-1936

In 1936 the Elim Movement celebrated its 21st Anniversary with a series of Coming of Age celebrations culminating in a day of meetings at the Crystal Palace, London, where more than 12,000 people gathered from churches across the United Kingdom.

In addition, a seven week tour took George Jeffreys and his team to 35 churches across the UK and to special services in Belfast's Kings Hall where 750 received Christ in three weeks. The 1936 annual Royal Albert Hall meetings were enhanced by 13 other simultaneous events. Many who gathered in those celebrations could testify to their conversion, many to personal healing and to the transforming impact of the gospel and power of the Holy Spirit. They had become part not just of a local congregation, but of a swelling movement of thousands of spirit filled believers eager to reach the whole nation for Christ.

One such person was Henry Hake who won that year's 52 mile London to Brighton walking race. He had been a heart patient until healed at a meeting at the Surrey Tabernacle in 1925. He went on to win the same race five times in eight years and regularly testified that Jesus had healed him.

In all the events throughout the UK they sang and they rejoiced, they worshipped and they witnessed. At the Crystal Palace Elim members, choirs and music bands told the story of those 21 years in a two and a half hour dramatic presentation, including sound effects.

At the Royal Albert Hall event 44 cancer cases, 14 blind people and more than 50 others testified to physical healing. At the close of the meetings, 10,000 people from the top balcony to the boxes and stalls waved their large gold, red, white and blue hymn-sheets to the rhythm of the songs.

GREETINGS FROM THE FOURSQUARE GOSPEL DEMONSTRATION AT THE CRYSTAL PALACE

Walking in Victory

*H*enry Hake was the only man ever to win the London to Brighton Walk five times. His fifth victory occurred on Saturday, April 30, 1936, when he broke the existing record by covering the fifty plus miles in 8 hours, 36 minutes 14 seconds. His achievements are even more amazing as thirteen years before he was hopelessly ill.

The June 1938 *Elim Evangel* records his achievement and healing. In 1923 Henry experienced symptoms of a mystery sickness which was diagnosed as a rare complaint (achalasia of cardia) which, despite treatment became worse. Three times Henry was admitted to hospital. Doctors tried all they knew but by April 1925 Henry was facing life as a chronic invalid. In desperation on May 8, 1925, he attended a meeting at the Surrey Tabernacle where he was prayed for and miraculously healed.

In order to build up strength after his healing Henry took up walking, first strolling gently to increase his stamina then, as he became stronger, he became more enthusiastic. By 1929 he could walk 40 miles a day.

Henry said of his healing, "Everyone said I should always be a weakling and must take a lot of care of myself. It seemed to me that if the vicious circle which was slowly crushing me were reversed – and it had been – then surely the action would lead cumulatively to real health. Moreover, if the Son of Man had come that we *'might have life and have it more abundantly'* then the outlook was brighter than that forecast. The road back was long, but the evening of May 8, 1925, was the beginning."

In order to demonstrate the extent of his healing he took part in his first race which was 25 miles, finishing third. He decided to take up race walking and by 1935 was a national champion. He set a record by winning the London to Brighton race five times in eight years.

> " Does Divine Healing really work? I say emphatically it does! Almost hopeless in 1925, a National Walking Champion in 1935. Surely it speaks for itself and explains my enthusiasm for Divine Healing.
>
> Henry Hake

Rejoicing!

The 1920s and 30s were exciting times for the young Elim churches. Evangelism in all shapes and forms and fellowship was all part of the new church lifestyle.

Eastbourne's Crusader Choir in 1929.

The 'Happy Sheffield Gospellers' of 1937

A party of cycling evangelists in Sparkbrook Birmingham, 1938.

CHRIST IS COMING ARE YOU READY

YE MUST BE BORN AGAIN.

Other cycling bands were around the country and one in Brighton reported that they had had a "very successful season with nine souls saved at the open air meetings in the centre of town."

Committed to Worship

More than simply lively meetings and enthusiastic singing, the Elim movement has often been characterised by gatherings in which music and corporate worship is a vital part of the Holy Spirit's work. From mission halls to tent meetings to campaign meetings in the largest halls in the nation, Elim gatherings have experienced the tangible and manifest presence of God in vibrant and heartfelt worship. Moves of God have often been marked by new styles of worship and for the early Pentecostals their new found experience of the Holy Spirit overflowed into a theology and practice with worship at its very centre.

George Jeffreys had, as part of his Evangelistic Band, a gifted song leader – Ernest Darragh. The records of those early days tell of Jeffreys' powerful preaching but equally of Darragh leading the congregations in impassioned singing. From the rousing power of a classic hymn to the almost hushed whisper of a "prayerful chorus", Darragh led with a sensitivity to the presence and moving of the Holy Spirit.

This explosion of music was greatly enhanced by the Elim Publishing Company and Victory Press where a huge range of Elim recordings on vinyl records – first on 78rpm, then 33rpm – was produced. These included albums of the musical items from the campaigns as well as George Jeffreys preaching. It was, however, the publication of the Redemption Hymnal and the Elim Choruses which had the greatest impact on the worship life of churches and members. Initially published in paperback instalments, the Elim Choruses became an outlet for the new songs circulating the churches and being written by Elim people. They proved so popular that they were frequently republished until compiled into the Elim Choruses (nicknamed "the yellow chorus book").

The Redemption Hymnal ("the Red Hymnbook"), published in 1951, was even more successful. It provided a wonderful mix of the great hymns of the

Protestant and Evangelical tradition with the newer hymns of the Pentecostal experience. The hymns of Isaac Watts, Martin Luther, John Newton and Charles Wesley were intertwined with the new hymns of Harry Tee and E.C.W.Boulton. With a significant section of the hymnbook devoted to songs on the theme of the Holy Spirit this hymnal was a ground-breaking resource that influenced a generation of post war British Pentecostals.

Ernest Darragh

> " They do not come so much to church as to a meeting – with each other and with God, and their expectation is that God will come and meet with them.
>
> Dr Keith Warrington,
> Regents Theological College

"In Spirit and in Truth"

In the early Elim churches springing up all over Britain, there came a huge appetite for the worship experience people encountered in the great crusade meetings to happen in their local churches. Often borrowing tunes from the music halls and the popular songs of the day, they commissioned the writing and publishing of new songs, they organised choirs, orchestras and brass bands. They developed singing ministries – soloists, duets and quartets – which could provide an ongoing stream of praise in local churches.

Gloucester Mandolin Band 1938

The centrality of music and worship to the life of the Elim movement was marked by Douglas B. Gray being appointed as the Music Director of the Elim Churches. In January 1929 Gray, who was working at the Elim Offices in Clapham, had founded the London Crusader Choir. For the next fifty years Doug Gray led the choir as it became one of Britain's best known and widely travelled Christian choirs, singing and travelling throughout Scandinavia, Europe and North America.

Doug Gray

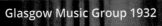
Glasgow Music Group 1932

The London Crusader Choir at the Royal Albert Hall

E.J. Phillips

Ernest John Phillips was a leading figure in the establishment of the Elim movement. Next to George Jeffreys, E.J., as he was known, was the second most important leader and his legacy possibly contributed more to the moulding of Elim than even Jeffreys.

He was born in Hove, Sussex, in 1893, the second son of John and Emily Phillips, and descendent of an influential Jewish family. One of his ancestors was the first Jewish Lord Mayor of London. He had two brothers, Hubert and Frederic, who both served as ministers in Elim. His sister, Dollie, was one of Elim's earliest missionaries and served in the Congo.

It is thought that E.J. was converted in 1909 aged 15. Significantly, he spoke more about being baptised in the Holy Spirit.

The 'Cardinal'

He joined the Elim Evangelistic Band in 1919 after being healed of a severe throat infection. His only appointment as a pastor was to the Elim Church in Armagh. This city is the home of the Roman Catholic Archbishops of Ireland who are frequently appointed cardinals. Because of this, E.J. was humorously referred to as "the cardinal" by his fellow ministers and this was the name George Jeffreys almost always used when writing to him.

E.J.'s great skill was in the area of administration and legal matters, he was the architect of Elim's Constitution. He was a brilliant conference debater and his colleagues were certain that his speech to the 1934 conference, on a secondary doctrine that George Jeffreys strongly believed in, saved the movement from catastrophe.

A major division occurred in 1940 when George Jeffreys and a number of ministers and churches left Elim to commence a new denomination. E.J. then became the leading figure in the movement, although he was adamant that he would not take the position of President which Mr Jeffreys had relinquished. He remained as Secretary General of Elim until 1957 and on the Executive Council (Elim's National Leadership Team) until 1965.

A Visionary Leader

Some would argue that Elim exchanged a charismatic leader for an administrative constitutionalist, however, in a quiet and unobtrusive manner, E.J. Phillips was a visionary leader. It was down to his strong, steady and yet inspired leadership, that Elim continued to grow after the ravages of World War II and internal strife, and maintained its missional ethos.

He married his wife, Molly, on November 1936. He first proposed to her in 1926 and waited ten years for her to accept him. He died on September 5, 1979.

Ernest John Phillips

The Gathering Storm

The Coming of Age marked the peak of Elim's pre-World War II outreach and ministry. The following years saw significant changes; there were internal challenges on matters of organisation and doctrine, and in a nation heading towards War there were also external pressures in the spiritual climate of Britain which made pioneering new churches and widespread evangelism more difficult.

In 1937 E.J.Phillips, the key leader who managed Elim's offices and structures, was rushed to hospital with a collapsed lung. He spent many months recuperating during which the burden of administration fell on George Jeffreys. George was an evangelist, at his best in the field conducting pioneer missions. He was increasingly uncomfortable with, and overwhelmed by, the growing administrative demands of the movement. There were property issues, the needs of ministers and churches and the pressing challenge of raising finance for expansion and evangelism. Just before Christmas 1937, Jeffreys was also taken ill and forced to take four months to rest and recover. Twenty three years of tireless ministry had taken their toll. He recovered, but never regained the strength and vigour he knew in those early years.

Jeffreys' discomfort with the huge workload that accompanied the rapid expansion of the movement was made more acute by his changing views of church government. Influenced by visits to the Pentecostal churches in Sweden, where churches had a tradition of local independence, he took steps to change the way Elim churches were governed.

A New Constitution

In the early years, George Jeffreys had been the founder and face of Elim. By 1934 he had agreed to the setting out of the Constitution of the Elim Church. He had also agreed to share the leadership of the movement with an Executive Council of eight members plus himself as the chairman. The movement had become too large and far reaching to be governed by one man, however gifted and charismatic.

In late 1938 and 1939 at Elim's Annual Conferences, George Jeffreys brought a series of proposals for change. The Conference eventually agreed to each proposal but he was not satisfied. George threatened a number of times to resign and eventually did so. Against the backdrop of impending war Elim was plunged into a crisis from which it seemed for a while it might not recover. George Jeffreys not only left the Elim movement God had used him to found, but he actively sought to draw pastors and churches to a breakaway group he called The Bible Pattern.

Such testing, however, brought a new dependence upon God and a fresh unity. Internal division and strife took time to heal but the greater strains of a nation at war stirred Elim people to believe God for a fresh wave of outreach and mission – albeit to a transformed post-war nation.

George Jeffreys continued to preach and hold evangelistic meetings for many years but his ministry never again had the same impact. He died in his home in Clapham on January 26, 1962 aged 72. He was seen by many as the greatest British evangelist of his generation and had been used by God to bring multiple thousands to Christ and to birth a movement of churches that would carry the full gospel to future generations.

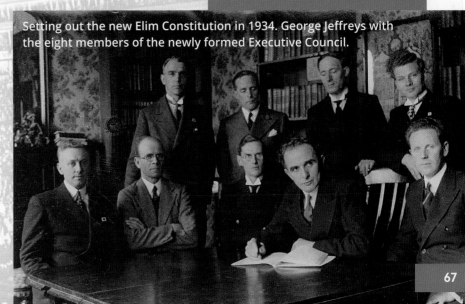

Setting out the new Elim Constitution in 1934. George Jeffreys with the eight members of the newly formed Executive Council.

The War Years
Suffering and sacrifice

On Sunday September 2, 1939, George Jeffreys was leading the service at Brighton Elim Church when the wail of an air raid siren interrupted the meeting. The next day war was declared on Germany. Over the next six years the nation paid a huge price in suffering and sacrifice. For Elim, the days of opportunity had ended. The vast crowds evaporated, town and city centres, often where Elim's strongest congregations were based, were evacuated. Elim's headquarters were transferred to Glossop, Derbyshire.

The air raids were particularly destructive with London the worst hit. Whole buildings were lost in Clapham, Islington, South Croydon, Canning Town, Stratford and Forest Hill. Further afield, Plymouth, Leicester, Gloucester and Southampton Elim churches received direct hits and were totally destroyed. Near misses meant churches in Hull, Ilford, Wimbledon, Exeter, Greenock, Liverpool, Aberdeen, Sparkbrook, Cardiff, Coventry and Yeovil required urgent repair work with whatever materials the congregation could get hold of. Some services continued with bombs actually falling.

Outreach to the troops

Some churches developed special outreach and ministry to the thousands of Forces men and women stationed nearby. Percy Brewster at Cardiff City Temple held meetings for service personnel throughout the war. One young man, John Lancaster, attended from the nearby RAF camp. He went on to become a much loved Elim pastor and national leader, particularly known as an outstanding writer, preacher and communicator. In Wales, six churches were opened as a result of war-time missions. John Woodhead in Carlisle saw around 4,000 decisions for Christ during the war. Archie Scott at Aldershot, Florence Munday at Gosport and Gerald Ladlow at Portsmouth all led their churches in focussed outreach to thousands of men and women. They reached out with friendship, food and spiritual help.

God's faithfulness

Elim was not immune to the ravages of war and every church was touched by its horrors and sorrows. Yet there were remarkable stories of deliverance and escape. In Gloucester, Pastor Leon Quest saw bombs drop from a German plane, rushed into the church and shouted for all to get under the benches. The building collapsed but no one was hurt.

In the aftermath of D-Day a young Scottish soldier and Elim member, Robert Campbell, jumped into a tank to rescue some men pinned down by enemy fire. He was wounded in the process and shipped back to Britain for treatment. Robert trusted God and was miraculously healed of his injuries in his hospital bed. His sons David and Ian Campbell both serve as Elim ministers today.

A young John Lancaster who served in Burma with the RAF.

Wartime destruction in Plymouth where the Elim church was completely destroyed.

"In one week a church might be reduced by nine tenths by the call up to the armed forces or to national service. In two terrible winters, 1940 and 1941, with relentless cold and snow for months, nights of terrifying bombing, the loss of loved ones, the threat of invasion, Elim meetings went on, choruses rang out, every chance for God was taken up and Elim refused to die. Some churches closed their doors for a time, but soon opened them again.

Elim Evangelist George Canty

Sunshine Corner

Ladies helping out with the cooking at a youth camp in 1944

Part of the huge crowd attending one of Archie Biddle's "Sunshine Corners".

Children and young people's work continued *throughout the war years.* In Rotherham, Yorkshire, the local authorities were very supportive of Pastor Archie Biddle when he arrived there in the latter part of the war. He ran Sunshine Corner meetings for children for 15 years drawing an average attendance of 3,000, and more on Bank Holidays. The local authority loaned loudspeaker equipment and a piano and put out 3,000 chairs each time.

Archie Biddle in Rotherham where the Sunshine Corner meetings took place.

Guernsey and the Jackboot 1940-45

Churches across the country were affected by their young men and women going to war, air raids destroying churches and people's homes, rationing, evacuation of children and the fear of what could happen. But no churches in Britain experienced the difficulties of wartime to the same extent as the three Elim churches on the tiny Channel Island of Guernsey.

The Elim churches on Guernsey went through five terrifying years of German Occupation. The Vazon Elim Church had been a Pentecostal Mission since 1911 and joined the Elim movement in 1921. Boosted in numbers by a crusade led by George Jeffreys in 1926 the growing church at Vazon began planting out congregations, one in the north of Guernsey at Delancey in 1934 and another in the capital St Peter Port in 1936. At the time they were the only Elim churches in the Channel Islands.

German soldiers marching in Guernsey

German Occupation

Pastor and Mrs Gilbert Dunk and their sons Michael and Philip

Nine months after the start of the War on Sunday June 30, 1940, Elim folk in Guernsey went into their gospel services as free British people and came out under Nazi domination as German forces invaded the island. The sermon preached that evening by Gilbert Dunk, minister of the church in St Peter Port was on 'hope'. Amazingly the work in Guernsey continued, despite the evacuation of around forty per cent of the island's population prior to this and the fact that the ministry team became severely depleted. Pastor John Woodhead of Vazon was away from Guernsey at the time of the invasion and could not return to the island.

Sacrifice

Arthur Jackson of Delancey was sent to a prison camp in September 1942, one of more than 1,003 men, women and children deported from Guernsey and Sark during 1942 and 1943 to Germany. Gilbert Dunk and his wife were only spared that fate because a Methodist minister, Rev Donald Stuart, offered to go to Germany in his place. Rev Stuart and his wife had no children and he was close to retirement, his act of sacrifice which allowed Gilbert Dunk to stay with his young family, led to Rev Stuart's death from malnutrition in Germany. Pastor Dunk became the minister of all three churches and led them through five years of isolation, oppression and fear.

A sketch of Arthur Jackson by a fellow prisoner.

> **"** Pastor Jackson left us for Germany on September 27, 1942. I lost a fine colleague and a great friend but God used him in the camp to which he was sent.
>
> Gilbert Dunk.

Pastor Jackson survived the war and returned to Britain but was too unwell from his ordeal in the German prison camp to continue in ministry.

New Zealand

Following his leadership of the churches in Guernsey during their time of German occupation, God took Gilbert Dunk and his family in a new direction – to New Zealand. The Pentecostal Church of New Zealand (PCNZ) was formed in 1922 after a visit by Smith Wigglesworth. There were miraculous healings and hundreds of people saved in a mission conducted by him at Wellington Town Hall. The work spread to other towns and as a result a second visit was arranged for the following year. This was the beginning of the Pentecostal Church of New Zealand (PCNZ). At a conference in 1949 PCNZ agreed to link up with the Elim Church of Great Britain with a view to establishing an Elim work in the country. Pastor and Mrs Gilbert Dunk transferred from Britain to New Zealand and landed in Wellington in April 1952 and the Elim Church of New Zealand (Incorporated) was launched in 1953. Today the Elim Church of New Zealand comprises more than 40 churches.

Pastor Jackson

Pentecostal in Spirit

Through four long hard years of suspicion, intimidation and starvation the Elim churches and people drew close to one another and to the Lord. Baptismal services were held for new converts. Occasionally German soldiers would appear at church meetings causing quite a bit of fear among the locals. One such turned out to be Herman Lauster, a German Pentecostal pastor, who had been forced into an artillery unit as an alternative to jail by the Nazis. He secretly baptised a number of his fellow soldiers in the sea and used to meet with Elim members for house group Bible studies.

Herman Lauster (main picture, third from right), a German Pentecostal pastor, was one of the German force occupying Guernsey. With him are believing soldiers, probably Army cooks, and Herman's converts and a local Elim family.

❝ I have sweet and happy memories of the company of three dear brethren in the German army.

Gilbert Dunk the minister of the Guernsey churches during the time of German occupation of the Channel Islands

Liberation

Liberation finally came on May 9, 1945, following Winston Churchill's radio declaration that "our dear Channel Islands are to be freed today". Scenes of inexpressible joy greeted the liberating British troops who could hardly march along the town seafront due to being mobbed by jubilant islanders. As he stood in the crowd watching through tears of relief, Gilbert Dunk was embraced by a local preacher who said, *"This is the Lord's doing and it is marvellous in our eyes"*. Guernsey's years under the heel of the jackboot were at an end.

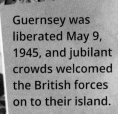

Guernsey was liberated May 9, 1945, and jubilant crowds welcomed the British forces on to their island.

Other countries where there were Elim churches were affected by the war. A work in Belgium had been started in April 1937 by Archie Scott. He originally wanted to go to the Belgian Congo and studied French in Liege. When the door to the Congo closed he stayed in Belgium where God led him to La Louviere, a town where the Gospel had never been preached. The following year, another work was started in Haine St Pierre. When the country was invaded in 1940 Archie Scott and his family fled back to England, just escaping the advancing German Army. Four years after Belgium fell, and as Europe was being liberated, the Elim Foreign Missions Council was wondering how the churches had fared during the German occupation. Fred Harrison, a Crusader from the Elim Church in Bradford, and driver of Field Marshal Montgomery's staff car, was at the liberation of Haine St Pierre and was greeted by a young girl who recognised his Crusader badge on his army uniform. The churches in Belgium had survived. In 1946 Tom Evans, his wife Eva and two children went to Belgium and since then the work has continued with missionaries such as Mike and Collette Williams, Phil and Barbara Gray and Leo and Hazel Maeckelberghe serving the country.

P.S. Brewster
Evangelist, minister, mentor and spiritual statesman.

Post War Expansion

The War Years changed the spiritual climate of the nation. The effects were felt across the Elim movement way beyond the impact of bombed buildings and displaced members. The war had begun with a parting of the ways between Elim and George Jeffreys.

Yet over those trying years, Elim churches had survived and developed a resilience and strength that caused them to come out of war into the austerity of post-war Britain with renewed focus. Though outwardly they felt weak and ill equipped for evangelistic outreach, inwardly they began to turn again to prayer and planning fresh waves of mission to towns and communities which, though hardened by the ravages of war, were more in need of the gospel than ever.

In time a stream of pastors and evangelists rose to this challenge, but initially the Lord raised up P.S. Brewster. Elim had been birthed through the apostolic ministry of evangelist George Jeffreys, then strengthened and developed by the leadership gifts of E.J. Phillips, now it was propelled forward by the strategic ministry and example of P.S. Brewster.

Pastor, Evangelist, Statesman

Born in the East End of London in 1908, Percy Stanley Brewster became one of the most gifted evangelists of his generation. Known affectionately as "P.S." to his friends, "Mr Brewster" to younger ministers and "Pastor Brewster" to his loving congregation, for almost half a century he was used by God to lead city churches in Wales, to pioneer scores of new churches across the UK and as a Pentecostal leader and statesman to exercise a worldwide ministry and influence.

Converted at the age of 20 at George Jeffreys' campaign at Ilford Town Hall in 1928, P.S. Brewster was soon made the youth leader at the Elim church in East Ham. He left the building trade to enter the Christian ministry and was one of the first crop of converts from George Jeffreys' evangelistic missions to take up the call to reach towns and cities for Christ.

After a brief period at the Elim Bible College he was asked to help follow up Jeffreys' huge city wide crusade in Birmingham in 1930. His first appointment as a minister was at the Swansea City Temple. Pastoring an established and thriving church in Swansea, Brewster was burdened for the nearby town of Neath. It was here that his developing gifts first began to find expression in evangelism and outreach.

In 1935, following a vision in which he saw a hall packed with people, he found a venue and booked it. It was the exact hall he had seen in the vision. Brewster preached the gospel, prayed for the sick and saw many respond to Christ and some healings. The new Neath Elim church was opened shortly afterwards and P.S. Brewster began to recognize that God had put within him a mix of pastoral and evangelistic gifts which would be a pattern for his lifelong ministry.

Cardiff and Beyond

In 1939, P.S. Brewster was asked to take on the leadership of the City Temple, Cardiff. At the time this was Elim's largest church and occupied a newly opened 1,000 seater building on the edge of the city centre.

He came to the city at the start of World War II, during which he steered the congregation through some dark days, including the building being bombed, but he came to love the church and city and made Cardiff his home and the church his springboard for mission and church planting for 35 years.

After the war he began to plan evangelistic "crusades". Hiring church buildings, cinemas, concert halls and, if none of these were readily available, pitching a large tent, P.S. would preach the "Foursquare Gospel". He held campaigns and opened churches in Brecon, Bridgend, Pontypridd, Caerphilly, Porth and a host of other towns throughout the valleys of South Wales. In England he went on to open churches in Bristol, Exeter, Newcastle, Derby, Hereford and Oxford. More than 40 churches were planted by P.S. and his teams of volunteer workers mainly drawn from Cardiff plus a growing band of trainee ministers and evangelists.

Developing Evangelists

It was in the Exeter crusade that a young Wynne Lewis first cut his teeth in evangelistic ministry. In later years Wynne led Kensington Temple in London through a decade of amazing church growth from a congregation of 600 to over 5,000. He spoke of P.S. as his mentor and inspiration.

P.S. Brewster had an ability to see the hand of God upon a person's life. A young Scots evangelist, Alexander Tee, was one whom Brewster brought to assist him at Cardiff. At P.S.'s side Alex developed an evangelist gifting which birthed a city wide youth ministry reaching a thousand young people a week. Alex Tee left Cardiff to plant many churches and lead multitudes to Christ. Similarly, he encouraged Louie McKendrick, a young woman in the church who worked for the Royal Institute for the Blind, and had great administrative skills. He gave her the task of organizing new youth branches which within a few years impacted hundreds of people.

Laying the foundation stone for the Caerphilly Elim Church.

Worldwide Ministry

In the 1950s and 60s P.S. became a keen student of the work of the Holy Spirit around the world. Travelling to the USA he saw the impact of Sunday Schools and youth ministry and came back to Cardiff committed to pioneering new methods to reach children and youth. So, in the late 50s he began a bus ministry which brought crowds of young people in from the new housing estates and opened youth branches in almost every school in the city.

He regularly produced magazines and brochures. He brought the world's best preachers, singers and Christian leaders to Cardiff. A young Dr David Yonggi Cho first came to the UK at Brewster's invitation. Then pastoring a church of 10,000 in Seoul, South Korea, Cho often returned to minister alongside his friend but not without chiding the church for not having grown since his last visit.

In the last two decades of his life this extraordinary blend of pastoral and evangelistic ministry opened many doors. He served from 1952 on the Elim Executive Council, becoming the leader of the Elim Pentecostal Churches in 1974. He also served on the council of The Pentecostal World Conference, was Editor of *World Pentecost* magazine and, in 1976, was presiding host for the Pentecostal World Conference at the Royal Albert Hall, London. These years saw him travelling the world preaching and ministering on "The Spreading Flame of Pentecost". He died in London in 1980 after a short illness and is buried in Cardiff.

THE STRONGEST MAN IN CARDIFF'S RELIGIOUS LIFE
The Rev. Brewster draws 1,000 people to the neon-lit City Temple every Sunday. He anoints the sick with oil. Those who have been cured give testimony. Choruses like 'Victory in Jesus' almost lift the roof. But many churchgoers have no taste for 'hot' religion, describe his technique as 'theatrical.'

News of missions in South Wales were reported regularly by the press.

Crowds queuing for P.S. Brewster's 'Great Public Revival and Divine Healing Crusade' in Newcastle, 1957, where there were 940 professions of faith in the first week and many accounts of miraculous healings. A thriving church was established through the meetings.

Dr David Yonggi Cho with Pastors P.S.Brewster, Ramon Hunston and Jim Dick.

The Men and Women who helped shape Elim

Elim emerged from World War II with a deeply felt gratitude to God for bringing the nation, and so many Elim churches and people, through the horror of wartime. Yet the leaders' overriding concern was to return to the priority of evangelism.

An Evangelistic Committee was set up in 1946 "with the sole purpose of furthering and intensifying evangelistic efforts." Ministers, such as P.S. Brewster, John Woodhead and George Canty, led the way. P.S. Brewster wrote, "Some of us believe that Elim was raised by God to meet an urgent need. This movement has operated, and is operating, and must continue to operate to meet this vital need." The tent campaign that P.S. held in Wigan in 1945 leaving behind a thriving church was the first of a new wave of such evangelism.

A 1946 booklet, Labourers With God, written as an introduction to the Elim movement, declared that "the main function of the District Presbytery is to extend the work of Elim in the District." By 1960, the Evangelistic Committee had identified "New Towns," built to house the thousands displaced and homeless due to wartime bombing, as ripe for evangelism. This was not just a strategy initiated from Elim's Head Offices, rather, it was encouraged at ground level – in local churches and District Presbyteries.

Over the next 20 years Elim evangelists planted numerous churches in cities, towns and communities where there had previously been little or no Pentecostal witness.

John Woodhead

John Woodhead from Mosborough, Yorkshire, became one of Elim's most fruitful ministers. Married to Alice, they had two daughters, Eileen and Dorothy. Eileen was the mother of the present General Superintendent of Elim – John Glass.

During World War II Woodhead ministered to the troops whilst pastor in Carlisle and was able to empathise with the soldiers as he had been wounded in action during World War I. He combined an evangelistic ministry with his pastoral work and led some of Elim's largest churches. He became President of the Elim churches in 1960 and served on the Executive Council for two years.

Wynne Lewis commented on John's bravery whilst conducting missions in the East End of London. During these meetings he was set upon and dragged off the platform but refused to be intimidated. George Canty, his pianist on that mission, had a wooden mallet by the side of his piano, ready to repel further invasions. As a pastor-evangelist, his churches thrived and his members caught their pastor's enthusiasm for evangelism.

John's last pastorate was in York. He retired in 1962 and died in 1977.

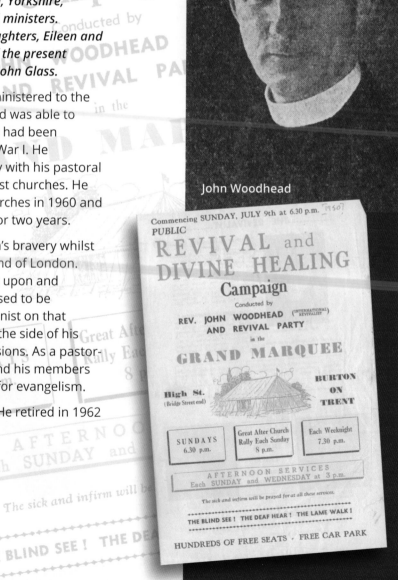

John Woodhead

Harry William Greenway

Harry William Greenway (Billy to his friends) was one of Elim's most respected leaders and a key figure in the development of the Elim Movement.

He initiated the Trafalgar Square open air meetings on Easter Mondays prior to the great Royal Albert Hall celebrations and conducted the meetings for 27 years. He was a member of the Evangelistic Committee where he formed a close association with P.S. Brewster.

W.G. Hathaway

William George Hathaway was born in 1892 and became a leading figure within the Elim Movement.

After serving with the United Apostolic Faith Church in Scotland, he came into contact with George Jeffreys and Elim during the mission that was held in Glasgow in 1928.

He was deeply impressed by Jeffreys and joined Elim and was appointed minister of the Clapham church in July of that year.

He was a gifted musician and hymn writer.

Sunny Blundell

In the 1940s, 50s and 60s, children's meetings and Sunshine Corner in particular were a regular part of most Elim churches. A song about it went,

> *Sunshine Corner all is very fine,*
> *It's for children under ninety nine.*
> *All are welcome, seats are given free,*
> *Elim Sunshine Corner is the place for me.*

In the austerity that followed World War II, *Sunshine Corner* was an oasis of fun and activity where many children came to faith in Jesus Christ.

Sunny Blundell-Connell was a children's evangelist with the Elim Church. Born in 1904, in Prescott, Lancashire, she was named Ivy until the first day after her conversion when she took the name "Sunny". At the time, during World War II, she was enlisted in the ATS (*Auxiliary Territorial Service,* the women's branch of the army). She wrote in a book about her conversion experience of a young Christian woman who worked alongside her in the army and who invited her to church.

Sunny became a member of the Elim Church in Salisbury and entered the Elim ministry in November 1945 leading a number of Elim churches including a mission hall in Glasgow. She had a great passion for reaching children with the Gospel and developed a highly visual method of communicating through flannel-graphs. This was "state-of-the-art" in the days when few people had televisions and not all children could afford to go to the Saturday matinee at the local pictures.

Her performances were electric and adults as well as children were mesmerised by her infectious humour and natural gift in communicating. Her ministry affected the lives of thousands of children and a number of ministers made their first commitments as Christians in her meetings.

On leaving the Army, Sunny made a comment in the discharge book,

" After six years in His Majesty's Forces, I am going out a better woman than when I joined up, for since then I have met the Lord Jesus Christ and been gloriously saved. Hallelujah!

(Ivy Blundell, No. 22856 Quarter-Master Sergeant)

TO-DAY IN THE ROYAL ALBERT HALL
2.30 AND 6.30
TWO GREAT ELIM MEETINGS.
THOUSANDS OF FREE SEATS

For twenty seven years Elim held Easter Rallies in the heart of London at Trafalgar Square prior to the afternoon and evening meetings at the Royal Albert Hall. Tens of thousands of Elim people attended as the Gospel was preached in the heart of the city. Pictured: Brian Garrard preaching at Nelson's Column.

The New Generation
The 60s and 70s

The 1960s were a time of great change in Britain. The post-war baby boom generation was growing up in a world which seemed to be shaking off the drabness and austerity of the 50s and embracing what looked like a new world of endless possibilities. It was a colourful time – the era of the Beatles, the Rolling Stones, Carnaby Street and protests over the Vietnam War. The world suddenly seemed to revolve around the new "younger generation", many of whom had very different lifestyles and ideas to their parents.

Across the denominations many who had filled the churches during the war as they prayed for peace and victory now began to drift away looking for other answers to their life needs.

As the country began to recover economically from war-time restrictions, the Elim movement began its own recovery. The number of churches had grown steadily from 220 in 1948 to break the 300 barrier in 1962. Yet, the growing spiritual malaise of the times stirred Elim leaders and churches out of any sense of complacency. A special Prayer Conference was held in Birmingham in 1961 to respond to the changing moral and spiritual climate. An Evangelistic Commission called the same year sought to raise up a fresh wave of pioneer evangelism and mission particularly to the cities and the new towns that were springing up all over Britain. Sensing the need for a more radical and focussed approach, the Evangelistic Commission set researchers

to work to identify the towns and communities without an Elim church. They also called together those with evident evangelistic gifting and experience of pioneer ministry, such as Alex Tee and George Canty, and made them available to churches and groups of churches in a particular presbytery or area.

Crowds gathering to worship at a Trafalgar Square rally

The Class of '69

In the late 1960s whilst so many young people were caught up in the lifestyle of the period, Elim saw a surge in the numbers of those applying to train for ministry. In the space of just a few years one of Elim's most fruitful groups of leaders studied at the Elim Bible College and they went on to have a profound influence upon the Movement both at home and abroad. Leaders such as John Glass who would become Elim's General Superintendent, Regional Leaders Gordon Neale, Geoff Feasey, and Mike and Elisabeth Sherwood, Ruth and Lionel Currie who served in Ghana and Roy Lynn, martyred in the Vumba in 1978. Other names will be familiar as having faithfully pastored churches through the years including Maldwyn Jones, Cameron and Betty Crawford, Phil and Sally Thompsett, David and Margaret Kilpatrick, Paul Epton, Claude Ellerington, Adrian and Pauline Hawkes, Bob MacDonald, John and Iris Bristow, David and Maureen Butcher, Phil Parsons and Phil Niblett.

The Move to Capel

Elim Bible College at Capel, Surrey. Hundreds of ministers and missionaries were trained here and a language school was also developed which helped to train overseas students.

Evangelistic missions were part of training for the ministry and innovative ways of advertising the meetings were regularly used.

*A*fter 40 years in Clapham, the Elim Bible College moved to a former mansion in Capel, Surrey, in 1965. New facilities gave tremendous opportunity to Elim to train more and more leaders for the years ahead. The college has had many principals over the years, the longest serving being Wesley Gilpin. Wesley became Dean of the College in 1958. He transferred to Capel to lead the College into expansion. The one year course was extended, first to two, then three years. Staff numbers were increased and student enrolment grew steadily. Wesley brought a growing rigour and robustness to the theological training at Capel but balanced this with a keen pastoral concern. He served as Principal for 21 years, retiring in 1981. His students became leaders not only in Elim but in Pentecostal ministries and churches in many countries, including Switzerland, Canada, New Zealand and numerous countries in Africa.

Broadcasting to the Nation

Ron Jones leading at the Royal Albert Hall

*B*y the mid 1960s, Elim had been asked to broadcast services to the expanding TV audience. In 1965, Elim's then Secretary Genera H.W.Greenway and a young Pastor Eldin Corsi led the first Pentecostal Communion service to be broadcast on British Television from Kensington Temple. Elim Bible College student came up from Capel for the service and the controversial element for the watching audien was that speaking in tongues was heard in the meeting.

The mid 1970s saw a number of churches regularly recording and broadcasting on the radio. Notably, the *Cardiff City Temple Youth Ch* and the Bristol City Temple Choir *The New Creation Singers* produced popular albums and featured in many local and national events. Pastor Ron Jones who led the Bristol Church fo many years and went on to become Elim's Secretary General was at the forefront of a fre release of worship and music across the wider Elim movement.

COME ALIVE!
Cardiff City Temple Youth Choir
as featured on the BBC Sunday morning 'Come Alive' programme

PILGRIM

A Fresh Spirit of Worship

Len Cowdrey

David Woodfield

*T**he 1960s and 70s brought about a profound social revolution, not least in the new music sweeping the world.* Against this backdrop, Elim churches sought not to merely respond to fads and fashions but to continue to respond to the biblical invitation to worship God in ways which were fresh for each generation.

Though this was a period when Elim's services were dominated by the "Red" hymnal and Elim Chorus Book, Elim welcomed music ministries from overseas. Singers and musicians like Birgitta and Swante from Sweden, Big John Hall and Living Sound from the USA ministered with great impact.

The late 1970s and 80s saw the beginning of the contemporary worship movement with a host of singers and musicians beginning to write new songs – often for the guitar and worship band rather than piano and organ. There came a move from convenors to worship leaders who were themselves musicians and singers. Many churches began developing worship and music ministry.

Many churches began to experience a new freedom in worship. In the early 1970s, David Woodfield at Selly Oak and Len Cowdrey at Portsmouth saw significant moves of God accompanied by fresh and creative music and worship.

Gill Price and choir
at the Royal Albert Hall

A New Generation of Evangelists

Evangelist George Canty

*T*he 1960s also saw new evangelists come to the fore – men like Alex Tee and George Canty.

Scotsman Alex Tee went to Cardiff and for four years worked in the City Temple with Pastor P.S. Brewster. During that time God was preparing him for the work of an evangelist. Through Alex Tee's evangelistic campaigns more than twenty Elim churches were planted across Britain. In later years Alex partnered with Paul and Margaret Hallam (his son-in-law and daughter) in opening scores of churches and Bible Schools in Kenya and India.

George Canty was a dynamic evangelist serving Elim for many decades.

Alex Tee as a young evangelist and years later conducting huge rallies such as this one in Sheffield (here with Swedish gospel duo Birgitta and Swante)

The Mission Field in Europe

*F*rom the earliest days of Elim, overseas missions has always been a passion. For many decades the focus was on the continents of Africa, South America and Asia.

In 1978, Lesley Wigglesworth, grandson of evangelist Smith Wigglesworth, retired as Elim Missions Director after more than 25 years in the role. The very weekend of the Vumba Massacre he handed over responsibility for Elim Missions to David Ayling. David had been the pastor of the Ulster Temple, Belfast, and was one of the most outstanding pastors, preachers and leaders of his generation.

Under David's leadership, Elim Missions began to look closer to home and Brian Edwards, pastor of the Derby Elim Church was asked to spearhead mission into Europe. Over the next few years, with the shadow of the Iron Curtain over much of Eastern Europe, Brian mobilised the resources of Elim to sow and to establish fresh churches and ministries on the continent.

In 1979 the Euroteams programme was launched. Euroteams involved scores of young people being sent in teams on short term missions with experienced UK Pastors into European countries for up to four weeks of front line activity and outreach in different cultures and languages. In Western Europe, Euroteams went to such countries as Belgium, West Germany, Greece and Spain.

They also had the opportunity to go into Eastern Block countries, behind the Iron Curtain; to East Germany, Poland and to Czechoslovakia. Growing protest and changes in these nations made it more possible for those from the west to visit and Elim Euroteams took the opportunity to bring practical support with food and clothing for Poland and, often at considerable risk, taking Bibles and Christian literature to the "underground" churches.

Following the sudden death of David Ayling in January 1983, Brian Edwards was appointed Missions Director, a post he held for the next twenty years.

A Euroteam on the streets of Belgium

Supplies packed to send to Poland

nSZZ Solidarność MAZOWSZE

David Ayling with a Russian delegate to the Annual Conference

Brian Edwards

Prayer, Passion and Pentecost

The early Elim pioneers were a generation fired with a passion to reach people for Christ. Major towns and cities the length and breadth of the nation were impacted as the gospel was preached in the power and dynamic of the Holy Spirit. This power was built upon a foundation of prayer. Men and women cried to God in prayer, often around the clock, for the salvation of unsaved people. Prayer became a key factor in the establishing of vibrant centres of Pentecostal witness. Records of the young churches show that while hundreds and thousands attended Sunday meetings, prayer meetings were just as well attended.

Churches that were birthed through the ministry of George Jeffreys and the Elim Evangelistic Band became centres of gospel outreach, and many of them could truly be described as *Houses of Prayer*. From the early days, prayer was considered a vital part of the local assembly of believers. Prayer was considered to be the force that energised the witness and testimony, not only of the fellowship, but also the lives of individual believers. Pastors and leaders encouraged their congregation to gather for corporate prayer. There would be the call to pray for individual needs, the life and witness of the assembly, but also the wider ministry of the Elim Movement particularly in respect of evangelism and International Missions.

Such gatherings also provided opportunity for people seeking their 'Personal Pentecost' – the Baptism in the Holy Spirit.

Prayer was also seen as a vital factor in the training of prospective ministers. Those seeking to be released into pastoral ministry were urged to ensure that attention was given to the development of a private prayer and devotional life.

One notable development in the prayer ministry of Elim occurred in the late 1970s with the birth of *The Elim Prayer Partnership*. The General Superintendent of the day, Tom Walker, invited one of Elim's retired ministers, Frank Lavender, to form a small prayer group that would meet in the basement office of the Elim Headquarters in Cheltenham. This group met to pray while the Executive Council held their meetings. They would pray for God to grant wisdom to the council in their discussions and decisions.

From these early beginnings, the National Prayer Partnership developed as hundreds of people joined and covenanted to pray not only for the work of Elim, but also national and global issues. Frank then joined the prayer groupings that were meeting in Parliament and ensured that the Elim Pentecostal Churches were represented in that strategic prayer environment. Following Frank Lavender's retirement from the role, Barry Killick took over as Chair of what became *The Elim Prayer Network*, followed in 2005 by Alistair Cole.

As Elim stands on the threshold of another century, prayer and mission are the key ingredients of spiritual renewal both in terms of the church and the nation.

> " The man who has prayed well has studied well. If ever you are going to be a success in the work of God you must take it upon your heart to be diligent in prayer.
>
> *Elim Preachers' Handbook*

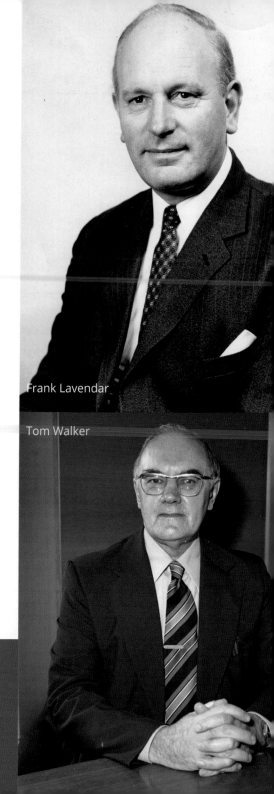

Frank Lavendar

Tom Walker

Catching the Pentecostal Fire

During the 1940s and 50s George Jeffreys continued ministering at home and abroad but his ministry never regained the height of popularity or numbers attending meetings that he had seen in his early days with Elim. He continued living in Clapham, London, where in 1961 he had a visit from a young evangelist who in time would impact the world on an unprecedented scale with the Gospel message.

Reinhard Bonnke, a young 21-year-old German Bible college student, had been studying at the Bible College of Wales in Swansea. While travelling back to Germany after completing his studies he stopped in London en route. Having time and some money to spare he decided to go on a sightseeing tour and ended up in Clapham Common. Deciding to take a walk the young Bonnke wandered around the streets at random until he came to a house with a nameplate that read 'George Jeffreys' on it. Wondering if it was the George Jeffreys that he had heard about he decided to knock the door and find out. At first he was refused entry by the housekeeper who answered the door, but then, from inside the house, he heard a voice calling for the young man to be let in.

Bonnke recalls of the meeting in his book *Living a Life of Fire*:

" I squeezed past that lady and as my eyes adjusted to the dim light, I saw him coming slowly down a staircase, holding it unsteadily. As he reached the landing, I stepped forward, took his hand and introduced myself. I told him I had a call of God on my life to be an evangelist and to preach the gospel in Africa.
What happened next was extraordinary. All of a sudden, he took me by the shoulders and fell to his knees pulling me to the floor with him. He placed his hands on my head and began to bless me as a father blesses a son, as Abraham blessed Isaac, who blessed Jacob, and on and on. The room seemed to light up with the glory of God as he poured out his prayer over me. I was dazed by that glory. I do not remember the words with which he blessed me, but I do remember their effect. My body felt electrified, tingling with divine energy.

After about a half hour he finished. I stood up and helped him to his feet. He seemed very frail. We said goodbye. The lady came and escorted him away. He could hardly stand. Nor could I, for different reasons. I stumbled from his house and staggered back toward Clapham Common like a drunken man. There, with my head spinning, I waited for a bus to carry me on my way to the railway station.

Bonnke returned to Germany and just three months later on January 26, 1962, George Jeffreys died. Reinhard Bonnke fulfilled his dream and calling to minister in Africa and in the decades following conducted meetings to crowds of more than a million people. Healings and salvations have followed in their tens of thousands. The legacy of George Jeffreys was the Elim movement and the thousands of others, such as Reinhard Bonnke, that he affected with his passion, anointing and desire to see a lost world touched with the love and compassion of Jesus Christ.

IN
MEMORY
of the
ELIM

MISSIONARIES
and their
CHILDREN

whose
lives
were
taken
in the
VUMBA
23rd
JUNE
1978

B.B.P.
24.9.1980

Elim's Darkest Day

Friday June 23, 1978, is remembered as the darkest day in Elim's history. On that day, twelve people were slaughtered at the Elim Mission station in northern Rhodesia (now Zimbabwe). Another died a week later. The sheer brutality of the massacre shocked the world.

At the time Rhodesia was in conflict; the forces of the government under Prime Minister Ian Smith opposing the so-called "liberation" forces led by Joshua Nkomo and Robert Mugabe (now President of Zimbabwe). The Elim missionaries were based at Katerere but the self-styled Patriotic Freedom Fighters were increasingly active in the area. Land mines made travelling hazardous adding to the difficult logistics of feeding the thousand people that the missionaries were responsible for in their school and hospital. They were also responsible for churches in the Katerere region.

In July 1977 after much consultation, and with all the Elim Missionaries strongly expressing that they did not want to leave

Peter and Brenda Griffiths and their two sons

the country, they moved 100 miles to the Eagle School in the Vumba, along with the majority of the school pupils. It was fifteen miles from Mutare, a short distance from the border with Mozambique. The Elim workers felt safe in their new location as the area was well protected. In the eleven months before the massacre four clinics were opened and pupils at the school progressed both scholastically and spiritually. Visits were made once a month to the hospital they had left at Katerere courtesy of the Missionary Aviation Fellowship.

Lesley Wigglesworth (Elim International Missions Director) and David Ayling, who became Missions Director after Wigglesworth's retirement, kept in close communication with the British Foreign and Commonwealth Office regarding the safety of their workers.

Ron Chapman, chairman of the work in Rhodesia, also kept in close contact with the church authorities and Elim Mission Board in Cheltenham, but events mounted as a number of Roman Catholic, Dutch Reformed, Salvation Army and American Southern Baptist workers were murdered. The killing of two Salvation Army female teachers in particular sent shock waves all over the world.

Alarmed by this news, it was decided the staff should move to Mutare and travel the fifteen miles to the school every day. The International Missions Board sent Peter Griffiths to Rhodesia in October 1977. Peter was the Principal of the Elim School there but he and his wife Brenda were in the UK on furlough along with Joy Bath, another missionary at the mission station. This brief visit resulted in the staff again expressing their desire to stay where they were despite the risks.

Lesley Wigglesworth

David Ayling

Ron Chapman

The Tragic Events of June 23

Despite the move to the seemingly safer area in the Vumba, 21 guerrillas came from over the border with Mozambique and attacked the missionaries one night with axes and other weapons. Eight adults and four children were killed, one baby was just three weeks old, the children were killed alongside their parents. A ninth adult, Mary Fisher, was cruelly attacked, but managed to run down the steep hill on which the school stood, going through agonizingly prickly bushes and trees.

She was found later and taken unconscious to hospital in the capital, Harare, where she died days later from her injuries. Mary should have been setting off for her furlough that day but her departure was delayed because she wanted to visit her sister who was on missionary work in Ghana before returning to Britain.

One of the guerrillas said later the murders were in retaliation for a Rhodesian Army attack on a guerrilla camp two years earlier, about which the missionaries knew nothing.

Father...forgive them

The shocking news devastated the entire Elim Movement. Politicians, churches and journalists all joined in the worldwide condemnation of the needless slaughter. As people across the world prayed for the families of those who died, many also prayed for forgiveness for the perpetrators.

On Sunday June 25, special services were held in Elim churches all over Britain. The Cheltenham Elim Church, next door to Elim International Offices, was packed for the Sunday morning service. Many representatives of the media were there. Some went into the service and came out astonished.

They could not get over the fact that the congregation, led by their minister Lionel Currie, was praying for the very people who had committed the murders as well as for relatives and friends of the deceased.

The media gave special attention to the prayer offered at Cheltenham Elim. The *Daily Mail* of June 26 carried the heading, *"Father...forgive them"*.

As a result of the attitude of forgiveness and prayer, the work of Elim in Zimbabwe continues to flourish with churches planted and schools and a thriving hospital.

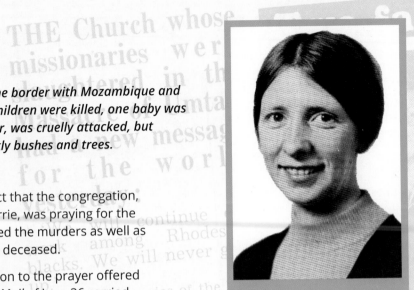

Mary Fisher

Prayers being said at the Memorial Service in Cheltenham Elim.

Prayers for Forgiveness Answered

We now know that the same prayer of forgiveness was prayed by some of the missionaries even as they were being killed. And it came to light that these prayers were answered – from the early 1980s several of those personally responsible for the killings were dramatically converted to faith in Jesus Christ.

After the massacre Peter Griffiths returned to Rhodesia. In January 1979, he was given a senior position in the Education Department in the newly independent Zimbabwe. The International Missions Board asked him to investigate what substance there was in rumours about the conversions. Peter was able to confirm what happened to a group in the platoon who were in an army camp in Entumbane shortly after the war had ended.

Peter was invited to go to a Pentecostal Bible College in Harare where he met the leader of the guerrillas who had killed the missionaries. The man had left school at 14 and had been the youngest platoon commander in ZANLA (Zimbabwe African National Liberation Army) operating then under the name of "War Devil", but he identified himself to Peter as Gavin. He came to faith through the work of a Christian lady in Bulawayo whom he had at first planned to kill. He was with many of the gang at the camp one evening waiting for her when they all saw a vision of the cross with God's hand pointing towards them in judgement. Several were converted that night and afterwards enrolled in Bible Colleges around Africa. Gavin was preparing for ministry as an evangelist, he had been so deeply moved by the way the missionaries had behaved at their cruel deaths that he was determined to preach the same gospel as they had.

In another separate incident, an African pastor named Mopofu, working for Harare Intercessors, was asked to speak at a rehabilitation centre for ex-combatants. While he was preaching, a paraplegic man screamed out, crying for mercy. He later confessed that he had been one of those responsible for killing the missionaries. He told the pastor how the missionaries had prayed for their killers as they were being slaughtered.

The missionaries are buried at Yeovil Cemetery in Mutare. Every year in June the graves are cleaned and flowers are put there.

National Memorial Service for the missionaries who died, Birmingham, 1978

The Missionaries and their children

Robert John (known as Roy) and Joyce Lynn

Roy and Joyce were both 36 when they were killed. Roy left for Rhodesia in 1975 after pastoring the Elim Church in Brookeborough, Northern Ireland, for over six years. Joyce was from York and a highly skilled nurse and midwife. They met in Rhodesia and were married in the UK on July 23, 1977. Their daughter, **Pamela Grace**, was born just three weeks before her tragic death. Joyce was the matron of the hospital.

Elizabeth Wendy H. White

Wendy (38) was from Kensington Temple, London, and was well experienced in nursing, teaching and social work. She served in Rhodesia for one year four months and was still on her first term when she was killed.

Peter and Sandra McCann

Peter (32) and Sandra (34) were both from Huddersfield, Yorkshire, and served in Rhodesia for almost eight and a half years. Peter was a science teacher and Sandra was very adept with needlework and handicrafts. Their children **Philip** aged nearly six and **Sharon** aged four and a half were killed with them. The McCanns had also lost a child during their missionary service who died in infancy whilst undergoing a minor operation.

The Cost of Caring

Joy Bath was an Elim missionary who served at the mission station in Katerere with many of those who died.

Joy, who came from a Christian home in Salisbury, was qualified as a nurse and midwife and felt the call of God to serve overseas going as a missionary to Katerere in July 1974. She returned to the UK to study at Elim Bible College ten months before the massacre and was at the college when the news broke of the tragic events of June 1978. After Bible College she was appointed to India to assist Olive Jarvis and Sylvia Beardwell in Dehri-on-Sone in Bihar, Northern India. She served there till 1985 when her visa was withdrawn and she had to return to the UK.

In 1987 Joy returned to the mission hospital at Katerere and served there until April 1992 when she was repatriated due to ill health. In looking after the mothers and babies in her care she had contracted AIDS, a disease which still blights huge parts of Africa.

For three years Joy lived with the understanding that unless God healed her the AIDS infection would take her life. On Saturday, April 15, just two days short of her 45th birthday Joy entered into the presence of her Lord and Saviour.

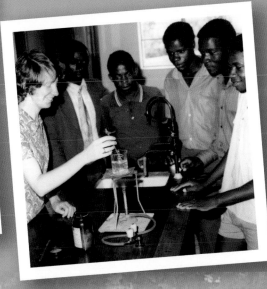

Catherine Picken

Catherine (55) was from Southend-on-Sea and was a proficient hockey player and sports teacher. She studied French and other subjects in Belgium for two years from 1956 in preparation for missionary work in Congo. She served there for one and a half years and had to escape at the time of the Katanga war. She served in Rhodesia for almost 18 years.

Philip and Susanna Evans

Philip (29) and Susanna (33) were from Nuneaton Elim. Their daughter Rebecca, just five, was killed with them. They ministered in Rhodesia for two and a half years and were still on their first term. Philip taught at the school and Sue was a qualified secretary. Their two other children, Timothy and Rachel, ten and eight, were away at boarding school at the time of the tragedy.

Mary E. Fisher

Mary was 31 when she died in hospital in Harare. Mary was from Caerphilly and taught maths and science. She went to Rhodesia in August 1973 and had served for almost five years. She had a rich soprano voice and her worship tapes were a great blessing both before and after her tragic death. She survived the initial attack, only to die from her injuries on June 30, 1978.

Zimbabwe — The Early Years

The first Elim missionaries to Zimbabwe (then Southern Rhodesia) were Mr and Mrs Jessie Williams who, in February 1949, left from the Elim Church, Graham Street, Birmingham, along with their seven year old son.

They were based at Penhalonga, twelve kilometres from Mutare, where they set up a church and school. The Williams faced numerous challenges including bouts of malaria and tick fever as well as damage to their newly constructed church building.

Early in 1951 the Williams were joined by Drs Cecil and Mary Brien. The Briens had been working near the Zambezi River for two years with an interdenominational mission. When Pastor Williams told the Briens about an unevangelized area in Nyanga District the Briens expressed interest in working there. Permission was granted by the region's District Commissioner to establish an Elim Mission in Katerere. The Briens pitched their tents and used them for accommodation and treating the sick by the Manjanja River, at the present site where Elim Mission continues to grow.

Later they built huts with straw roofs which they used as accommodation and a dispensary. During the early days Cecil Brien spent most of his time hauling materials, building structures and preaching while Mary carried out the dispensary work. Both Cecil and Mary were affected with malaria and illnesses several times. For many years the two dedicated doctors worked hard alone trusting God for resources to build a hospital, houses, to buy medicine and to sustain themselves. By the time the Briens retired in 1974 they had built 13 primary schools, Emmanuel Secondary School, a 75 bed hospital and a clinic.

Dr Mary Brien   Dr Cecil Brien

The Elim Hospital

The pupils of Emmanuel School today

The pupils of Manjanja Primary School

The Elim Work in Zimbabwe Today

To date the Elim Pentecostal Church work in Zimbabwe comprises 60 churches, one high school, two primary schools and the Elim Hospital.

Emmanuel High School, started in 1965, now has 344 girls, 298 boys and 32 teachers. Over the years the school has produced students who have graduated from universities filling key roles in the structure of the nation as teachers, lawyers, doctors, nurses, chief executive officers, pastors and theologians.

The Elim Pentecostal Church of Zimbabwe also runs Project 127, the name is taken James 1:27, "Religion that God our Father accepts as pure and faultless is this: to look after orphans and widows in their distress..." to support orphans and widows and help them out of poverty.

There is also the Elim Theological College which delivers a range of courses from Diplomas in Theology and Ministry to Certificates in Youth and Children's work training up workers and leaders for the local churches.

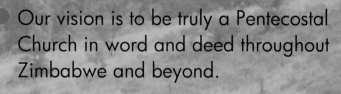

> Our vision is to be truly a Pentecostal Church in word and deed throughout Zimbabwe and beyond.

Rev Dr Pious Munembe, the General Overseer of the Elim Churches in Zimbabwe, who was a pupil at the Emmanuel School at the time of the Vumba tragedy.

The 80s and 90s

The Kensington Temple Story

The 1980s and 90s were decades of significant growth and spiritual breakthrough for Elim. The steady advance of the previous decades culminated in a dramatic move of God in London's Kensington Temple (KT) which inspired growth and fresh momentum throughout many churches in the movement.

In 1965, Eldin Corsie led a congregation of around 60 people from nearby Holland Park into Kensington Temple, a building that had seen a great move of God in the 1930s and had become known as "The Church of the Great Physician" due to the constant flow of miracles that took place there.

As the cleaning party worked its way through the building it found crutches and wheelchairs in the basement – reminders of past revivals. They had been discarded during the great healing meetings of George Jeffreys. The cleaners also found the "Church Full' sign that had often been seen outside the church. Eldin Corsie led Kensington Temple as Senior Minister for the next fifteen years and the congregation grew from 60 to 600 people.

Eldin laboured effectively in every area that was later to bear fruit in the 1980s. He placed a strong emphasis on prayer, welcomed members of the international community and exercised a strong evangelistic and teaching ministry. He laid the foundations for the multi-ethnic KT of today and his strong emphasis on prayer, evangelism and teaching is still characteristic to the church. He left KT in 1980 to become the Principal of Elim Bible College.

> A few weeks ago three people stood in the empty, dusty building and prayed that God would restore its former glory. One of the three was the secretary of the Elim Church at Holland Park, who in his youth had witnessed great scenes of revival there; where Sunday after Sunday the Temple was full to capacity and people were reluctantly turned away. These were years of plenty indeed!

The Kensington News and *West London Times* reporting on the reopening of KT

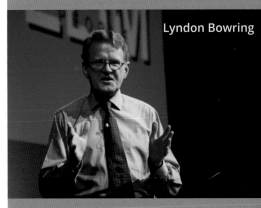
Lyndon Bowring

It was during Eldin Corsie's term of leadership that Lyndon Bowring, now the Executive Chairman of CARE, joined KT. He came with a team of students from London Bible College and served with the student team from 1971 to 1972. Lyndon was then invited to take up a full-time post at KT. He readily accepted the invitation. Lyndon was from an Elim church in Wales, so it was no surprise that he quickly felt at home and shortly afterwards became part of the pastoral team.

> Eldin was a man with the vision believing that God would re-establish His church because by the late seventies KT was the foremost Pentecostal church in the whole of the UK.

Lyndon Bowring

...ning of new church offices in 1982.
...m left, David Shaw, Wynne Lewis, Len Rammell and Eldin Corsie.

KT becomes "a mega church"

In September 1980, Wynne Lewis took over the leadership of KT. He hit the church "like a human tornado" as his leadership style, together with his ability to hear from God took the church forward. Under his leadership KT grew from 600 to 5,000 people. Much of the growth came from the international community but the real breakthrough came in 1983 after Wynne was laid up for many months following a car crash. God spoke to Wynne clearly about His intentions and when Wynne finally went back to work he was a changed person. He had a new anointing and the church began to grow rapidly. In 1985 Colin Dye joined the leadership team and founded the International Bible Institute of London. He also planted the first satellite church in Barnet in 1985. During the second half of the 1980s, missions took on a greater significance, as the KT leadership team became active in global evangelism. Since then, KT missions have taken people to Albania, Benin, Brazil, Croatia, Egypt, Finland, France, Sri Lanka, China and many other countries. In 1991 Wynne Lewis left KT for the post of General Superintendent of Elim, and Colin Dye was appointed Senior Minister. By now KT had around 50 satellite churches, and one fifth of KT's congregation was involved in church planting.

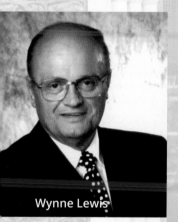
Wynne Lewis

Building a City Church

The 1990s was a decade of pioneering and steady growth. In 1993 Colin's book, *Building a City Church* set the vision for a revolutionary church model where KT and its satellite churches would function as one church to fulfil one vision - London and the world for Christ. As Kensington Temple London City Church (KTLCC) this was developed to become a network of churches, fellowships and ministries that achieved unity through diversity and released people into their ministry.

The many satellite churches and the central congregation had to come together somewhere, and the 1990s saw many great network-wide events that filled venues such as Wembley Arena, the Royal Albert Hall and the London Arena. In 1992 KT launched the first school of its kind in Britain, the School of Creative Ministries, and graduates of the new school were soon taking the Christian and secular media by storm. In March 1996 KT pioneered again, now in the area of TV ministry, as the 11am service was broadcast live to different venues in London, UK and Europe. The broadcasts continued over a number of years and KT held European-wide events, such as the Sword of the Spirit seminars by utilising satellite links. By the end of 2000, KTLCC consisted of 15,000 people, had planted around 150 churches and had more than 400 other groups and ministries under one umbrella.

Colin Dye

Opening and Dedication Services

> " We must see governing churches built with enough authority to transform society's institutions, claiming entire cities and nations back to God.
>
> Colin Dye

Transformation into a cell church

In September 2000 KTLCC took a bold step by restructuring the church along the lines of a cell model. The leadership of KT had become curious after seeing the incredible growth of its Spanish satellite church from 40 to 3,000 people in a period of only a few years through adopting a cell methodology. After a lengthy period seeking God, the KTLCC leadership was convinced that the cell church structure was the direction God wanted the network to take. KT embarked on a three year period of transition and by the end of the changeover KTLCC had more than 1,800 cell groups across London.

Over two decades the thousands of people involved in the KT story had been encouraged to believe God not only for a capital city but for towns, cities, communities and nations. In London, during this same period, many other churches began to see explosive growth including Elim churches in Ealing, City Gates – Ilford and the Camberwell Churches under the leadership of Pastor Sam Larbie. Growth in Elim was not confined to London as churches in other towns and cities also saw significant expansion. Many established Elim churches in centres such as

Plymouth, Glasgow, St Helens, Leeds-Bridge Street (ECI), Cardiff, Swansea and Bangor, N. Ireland and others saw remarkable periods of growth and blessing. This growth was often marked by seasons of the Holy Spirit's outpouring and creative outreach as such churches inspired others, shared resources and ministry and helped to establish a fresh climate of faith and expectation for what was to come.

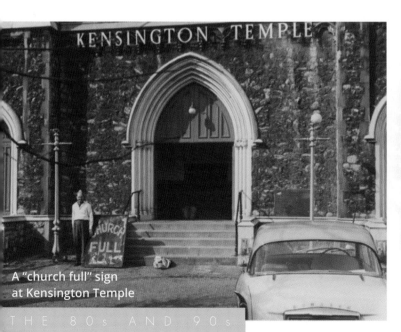

A "church full" sign at Kensington Temple

THE ILLUSTRATED LONDON NEWS

A NEWS HISTORY OF KENSINGTON TEMPLE

THE ILLUSTRATED LONDON NEWS
15th September 1849

HORBURY CHAPEL
"The rapidly increasing population of Notting Hill, and the plans laid out for new buildings in the surrounding district, for some time rendered additional religious accommodation desirable. Two large churches have been erected within the last few years; but these, with the Baptist and Wesleyan Chapels in the Kensington Gravel Pits and Queen's Road, did not suffice to meet the continually augmenting need for religious instruction in the vicinity. The nearest Chapels belonging to the Independent denomination are in Kensington and Paddington, but they are both at a considerable distance, and are already fully occupied. Under these circumstances, early in 1848 a committee of gentlemen, chiefly connected with the congregation assembling in Hornton Street Chapel, exerted themselves to meet the emergency of the case; and they commenced their good work, stimulated by a munificent donation of one thousand pounds. They next secured an eligible site at the corner of the Kensington Park Road and Weller Street East, and resolved to erect thereon a Chapel, capable of accommodating, upon the ground floor, about 700 persons. The first stone of the building was laid by Sir Culling Eardley, Bart, on the 30th of August 1848; and the Chapel was opened, with three services, on Thursday last..." ∎

Southport Conference 1984

" *H istory moves on small hinges. Small and apparently inconsequential acts of obedience and disobedience can change the course of individuals, churches and even Movements. One such incident occurred at a specially convened Elim Ministerial conference in Southport in 1984.*

What transpired was to overshadow the conference itself and prove pivotal in the Elim Movement for a generation following.

Some weeks before the conference a relatively unknown pastor of a church of around 60 people had a visitation from God. He was a converted gypsy and his name was Johnny Barr. Of this event he later wrote, "It was 2.45am on Thursday, April 5, when I was wakened from a deep sleep and heard the Lord say, 'Tell my people in the Elim Church Movement that they have three years to repent and put their house in order, otherwise I will remove their candlestick from its place.'"

John Barr

Johnny then contacted the Elim Headquarters, which at that time was in Cheltenham, and asked what he should do about the revelation. The person who took the call was John Smyth who occupied the role of Field Superintendent – a position in the Movement second only to the General Superintendent.

John suggested that Johnny should mention the vision at the upcoming Southport Conference. I was a minister in my thirties

at the time and was present when Johnny shared it with the assembled ministers. The atmosphere was understandably electric and within minutes all scheduled business was dispensed with as the implications of the message were assimilated and responded to.

The three areas mentioned were morality, party spirit and money.

After the conference concluded two or three ministers were to contact the Field Superintendent and confess that during a period in their ministry they had acted inappropriately and felt that the morality aspect of the message referred to them and consequently submitted themselves to discipline.

In the early 1980s there was a division within the Movement between what might be called traditional and radical leaders. The former were generally older in age and the latter younger – but not exclusively so. Some of those who were radical had expressed publicly disparaging remarks about those who they saw as "out of touch" and closed to change. Some of those in the traditional camp had spoken negatively of those they saw as divisive and unnecessarily causing trouble.

Within moments of the message being relayed both groups were apologising to one another with the radicals saying that they would not have a platform on which to speak had an older generation not had the willingness to sacrifice in the formative days of the Movement.

Those with traditional inclinations openly apologised for their inflexibility and unwillingness to listen to those who were beginning to see church in a new way.

John Smyth, Field Superintendant

"History does indeed move on small hinges"

This culminated by the Executive Council (the equivalent of the National Leadership Team) kneeling before God as younger leaders prayed blessing over them. I remember few ministry moments more moving or emotional than what occurred that day. As far as money was concerned, some sections of the Movement confessed to overstretching themselves financially in an attempt to expand and in some cases questioned whether their actions had been motivated more by pride than being directed by the Holy Spirit.

Fruits of repentance were seen by the ensuing sale of millions of pounds worth of assets in order to walk more humbly and circumspectly before God.

It is my belief that it is because of those actions that the Lord has allowed us, thirty years later, to be able to acquire the level of prime properties that we own today – always seeking to keep our heart and spirit right in the process.

One wonders what would have happened to our Movement if Johnny Barr had been too timid to pass on the revelation he had received in the belief that having too little status in the Movement he may not be listened to. Or what would have transpired if John Smyth had not had the humility to listen to the message on the basis that if God had anything to say to Elim he would have done so through senior leadership.

Fortunately both men were sensitive to the Holy Spirit and our Movement remains grateful for this.

History does indeed move on small hinges.

Tom Walker convening during the conference

One direct result of the Southport Conference was that fresh structures were put in place to enable the Movement to go forward. Most significantly, Elim introduced Regionalisation in order to strengthen the support and training of ministers on the ground and to provide a more local and region by region approach to planting and growing churches.

The first area to be regionalised was Scotland and in 1985 John Glass was appointed there as the first Regional Superintendent followed by Jim Dick and Kevin Peat. Some 30 years later we are thankful to God and the Scottish church leaders that the number of people in Elim churches in Scotland has risen significantly with new churches planted and a number of congregations having joined the Elim Movement over that period.

Following its successful launch in Scotland, Regionalisation was rolled out across the Elim Movement over the next few years.

Pictures from the 1984 Southport Conference

Conferences, Camps and Bible Weeks

Elim Conference 19

The early Elim pioneers set great store by large gatherings or "demonstrations" as they called them. In the best and most strategic venues in a town or city, Elim people gathered not just for themselves but as a witness to the surrounding community.

Camps, conferences and large gatherings have been a characteristic feature of Elim throughout its history. In later years, the venues changed as the purpose of gathering the wider Elim membership together was increasingly for teaching, business and for fellowship.

In the late 1960s the annual Elim Ministerial Conference was incorporated with a Bible Week and extended to the wider Elim membership. For over thirty years the Elim Conference had been primarily a "business" conference made up of Elim Ministers and appointed lay representatives from each church, usually meeting in a larger church or a hired hall. The advent of "holiday camps" in seaside towns around Britain opened up new possibilities to gather together for a week of fellowship, Bible teaching and worship whilst the ministers conducted the church business. First in Pontins Camp in Bracklesham Bay, then Blackpool, Morecambe and later at the huge Butlins camps in Clacton, Bognor Regis and Minehead, Elim gathered people in their thousands.

A growing feature of the Elim Conferences was the guest ministry as speakers from sister denominations in the UK and around the world were invited to minister as well as ministers and ministries from churches within Elim. Speakers such as Paul Walker and Jack Hayford from America were warmly received as were music ministries such as Birgitta and Swante from Sweden and Texan Big John Hall.

For many, Elim Conference will be remembered as a place of spiritual encounter. Perhaps it was the place they first responded to the gospel, were filled with the Holy Spirit or received physical healing. For some it was the place they met their spouse. For others the place where they felt the call of God to Bible College, to the mission field or to other forms of ministry.

Anne Graham-Lotz speaking at Elim Conference

Big John Hall

Birgitta

Life Changing Moments

Elim's Annual Conference
Butlins Clacton 1978

Fraisethorpe Youth Camp 1978

Ordination Services have
taken place at the
Annual Conference

Ordination Services have
taken place at the
Annual Conference

Elim youth and family camps have powerfully
benefited the movement for decades. Each year
thousands of families and young people attend Bible
weeks and youth camps in what, for many, are life-
shaping holidays. Many of today's Elim ministers and
leaders were saved, baptised in the Spirit or called
into ministry through an Elim camp. And they still
serve as places of fun, excitement, fellowship and
places where life changing experiences take place.

Bible study time at the Annual Conference
in Prestatyn, North Wales.

**‘ The impact on my life at that first
camp is hard to put into words:
except that it lit a fire in my heart
that has never gone out.**

Mervyn Tilley who went on from that experience
to spend a lifetime in ministry pastoring Elim churches
throughout the UK.

RIVERcamp – one of many camps
Elim churches host throughout the year.

A Special Relationship

John and Trish Waller

In the 1960s when Elim missionaries David and Margaret Mills were working in Ghana, an "accord" was established between Elim and the Church of Pentecost.

In 1989 a special agreement was signed between Elim and the Church of Pentecost (COP) which led to Elim offering assistance in the establishing of Church of Pentecost congregations in Britain. Initially, these churches were called ELICOP churches. They were linked fully with the Elim network in the UK and ELICOP ministers were ordained alongside Elim ministers at Elim's Annual Conference. Links were further strengthened as Elim sponsored COP ministers from Ghana to study at Elim's Bible College and through key leaders from Elim UK, such as Lionel and Ruth Currie and John and Trish Waller, serving in Ghana at COP's own Bible College.

We thank God for a true partnership which, more than 25 years on, has seen the Church of Pentecost plant over 120 churches in the towns and cities throughout the nation. They currently have more than 17,000 members in the UK and the Church of Pentecost has seen phenomenal growth not only in Ghana but across the many other nations where it has reached out in mission. They now number more than two million members worldwide with more than 140,000 new converts being added to the church every year.

Elim College Moves to Nantwich

Elim Bible College moved to Nantwich in 1987 after more than 20 years at Capel in Surrey and became Regents Theological College in 1996. The college then moved to its current site in Malvern in 2009.

At the Elim Conference in 1989.
Apostle and Mrs R. Ato Addison,(General Secretary of the church)
Lionel and Ruth Currie,Prophet M. K. Yeboah (Chairman of the church)

The Work in Ireland Develops

The 1980s onwards saw Elim in Ireland not only strengthen its churches in the North but significantly expand into the South. Serving as Irish Superintendent from 1979, Eric McComb retired in 2011 having brought a renewed vision for Elim to reach all Ireland for Christ. One feature of this was the building of many superb church facilities which combined excellent worship and teaching venues with facilities for youth, children and the wider community. New Superintendent Edwin Michael and the Irish Leadership Team are committed to Elim in Ireland building on its unique and extraordinary heritage with fresh faith and resources.

Eric McComb

The Elim Church in Monaghan

From early beginnings in a tent in 1915 to a new Elim church with facilities for all ages which serves the people and community of the town.

The Gathering Max at Birmingham's NEC

2000 and Beyond
Fresh Leadership for a New Season

*A*t the start of 2000 Wynne Lewis came to the end of his role as General Superintendent and John Glass took on the responsibility of leading Elim into the new century. John had a strong mandate from the movement to lead Elim forward and to identify and release the ministries and methods which would lead to even greater fruitfulness.

From the very beginning John began to emphasize the need for Elim not simply to look for numerical growth but to build and develop a culture within our churches of "Building Bigger People". John began to share the vision for a movement where thousands of Elim people and churches would be able to journey together into a future where expansion and growth was matched by spiritual depth and maturity.

Over the next few years John and the newly formed National Leadership Team (NLT) brought fresh vision and resources to established departments and ministries and launched new initiatives which would break new ground.

Direction Magazine

One of the first of these was a re-branding of *Direction* magazine. In partnership with New Life Publishing, the new look *Direction* used state of the art design and high quality production to encourage, teach and build up Elim people as well as offering an engaging and attractive introduction to church in general, to Elim and to the gospel.

Serious4God

In 2003 Mark Pugh, who at the time was on the ministry team at Birmingham Christian Centre, brought to the NLT a vision and a burden for re-establishing an Elim Youth Department. This resulted in the launch of Serious4God (S4G), a new national youth ministry with Mark as the Director empowered to envision and inspire churches to reach young people and to raise up dynamic youth ministry across the nation. In January 2014 Tim Alford took on the leadership of S4G.

Elim National Training

In 2004, Nigel Tween was appointed Elim's first National Training Director. The new Training department incorporated the Bible College (Regents Theological College) as well as a broader remit to develop a comprehensive training programme and culture right across the movement. For the next ten years, Nigel served as the Principal of the College while also shaping a range of training options which would be accessible and relevant to pastors, leaders and members on the front line of church life and ministry. At the centre of this was the NLT's desire to model and promote lifelong learning for all Elim ministers and leaders.

Through a wide range of training events, conferences and resources, Elim Training is investing in leaders and those with the calling and potential to lead and pioneer churches and to reach out in evangelism and mission.

> " Bigger people can be trusted with bigger blessings, greater responsibilities, larger challenges and, eventually, greater success — success that lasts.

> " God is not against 'Big'. God loves 'Big' and has called his church to largeness, favour and growth. But if there is one thing that God prioritises over big in the economy of His kingdom, it is 'deep'.
>
> John Glass

The Gathering Max – Birmingham's NEC Arena

*S*aturday October 27, 2007, is a date marked in Elim history as some 6,700 young people gathered from around the country for Serious4God's Gathering Max at the NEC Arena in Birmingham. The event featured The Gathering Band, Delirious?, 29th Chapter, Luv Esther and Mark Ritchie, and was broadcast live by GOD TV. The day ended with crowds of young people pouring forward to give their lives to Christ.

This amazing event was the result of a huge step of faith by Mark Pugh and the Serious4God team. With the full backing of the NLT they motivated hundreds of youth groups to come and to bring their unchurched friends believing God would do an extraordinary work in their lives.

Never in Elim's history have such numbers of young people come to faith in a single day! Many of those young people are now at the forefront of mission and ministry – in their local church, in college, in the workplace and some in full time ministry and leadership.

1137 young people made a public decision on one night

" The Gathering Max was the moment when numerous strands wove together. Churches stepped out booking tickets and transport, young people stepped out inviting friends and Elim stepped out booking a massive arena. I believe these steps were fuelled by the inspiration and provision of the Holy Spirit and the impact will be remembered by myself and many others for the rest of our lives.

Mark Pugh

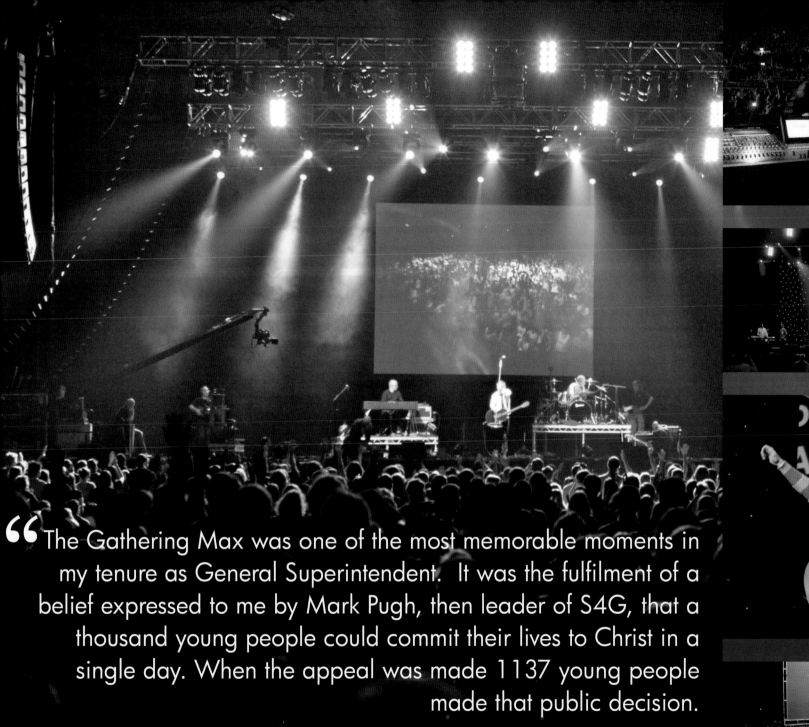

" The Gathering Max was one of the most memorable moments in my tenure as General Superintendent. It was the fulfilment of a belief expressed to me by Mark Pugh, then leader of S4G, that a thousand young people could commit their lives to Christ in a single day. When the appeal was made 1137 young people made that public decision.

John Glass

REACH – Elim's Department of Evangelism

In spring 2007, Elim's evangelism department was rebranded as 'REACH'. Its remit is to facilitate local church evangelism and church planting throughout the Elim movement. Gary Gibbs heads up a department seeking to come alongside local churches in order to provide support and encouragement for creative and fresh evangelistic outreach.

The New Landscape

At the turn of a new millennium, it was critical to recognise that the lifestyles, worldviews and philosophies of the majority of the UK population had undergone major change during the second half of the twentieth century. An accurate assessment of the new cultural landscape would be necessary in order to work out effective means of doing mission and planting new churches. Elim's re-branded REACH department is at the forefront of helping our churches navigate this new landscape with confidence and faith.

Aspire

In 2007 Elim launched Aspire – the first national women's ministry in Elim's history. Under the leadership of Marilyn Glass and a gifted team of experienced women leaders, Aspire began to build on the many good examples of ministry to and by women in our churches. From the outset its aim has been to care for and connect with women to encourage them to be all that God has called them to be and to equip them to fulfil His purposes.

Elim Sound

In a church scene richly blessed by a number of worship organisations, four men recognised the need for a collective praise identity within the Elim movement. Birthed in 2009 by worship leaders Sam Blake, Stephen Gibson, Joel Pridmore and Ian Yates, Elim Sound came about as a result of this need. Elim Sound gained much impetus from the launch of their Kingsway

released debut album Fresh Mercy in 2011 and the follow up album Sound of Hope in 2012.

Yet the real strength of Elim Sound lies not just in the ministry of the founders but in the network of worship leaders, musicians and songwriters in Elim churches all over the nation. Now Elim Sound is a maturing worship ministry which, through training, mentoring and nurturing young and less experienced worship singers and musicians, is having a significant effect on the worship life of churches.

Elim Sound

Malvern – A New Home for A New Season

During 2009, Elim International Offices and Regents Theological College relocated to the new Elim International Centre, West Malvern, set in 32 acres of land. This move brought Elim's administration, evangelism, missions, training, women's and youth ministries together under one roof.

The Big Centenary Ask

The BIG Centenary ASK

from John Glass

Elim

In 2011, a challenge was issued to every Elim minister and church to plant numerous new Christian communities and ministries through The Big Centenary Ask (TBCA). Looking ahead to Elim's centenary John Glass called each leader to prayerfully and practically consider planting or establishing a pioneer ministry. From the outset, this was not meant to be too prescriptive but to encourage leaders to explore ways in which they could plant a new church or a fresh missional expression of church in their local communities.

In the first year or so there were a number of new churches and exciting missional communities started. That trickle soon turned into a flood with dozens of church plants now established and numerous others in the planning or early stages. In housing estates, in cafes, in vacant church buildings, in cities, towns and rural hamlets these pioneer ministries are drawing a new generation to the adventure of front line mission. They are also releasing amazing creativity, passion and faith as new methods and approaches are put to the task of winning people for Christ in the needy communities of modern Britain.

MPower – Elim's Men's Ministry

Events like the Enable Men's Conference and many local church men's groups had shown for some time the appetite in our churches for relevant and inspiring ministry to men. In September 2014 Elim launched MPower, a new national men's ministry.

Under the leadership of Mark Lyndon Jones, MPower seeks to respond to the challenge of reaching and discipling men by harnessing the thousands of Elim men to believe for God to use them powerfully in the coming years. Engaging men to do "life together" as brothers in Christ will benefit their families, churches and communities through a growing a confidence in Christ which we believe MPower will offer through mutual encouragement, equipping and resourcing.

Partnering With Other Streams and Denominations

*W*hereas in its earliest days Elim and other Pentecostal churches faced much opposition from historic denominations for their bold and public presentation of the full gospel message, we now see a church landscape where Pentecostals are not grudgingly accepted but welcomed.

As well as developing strong fellowship links with other Pentecostal groups in the UK and overseas, Elim has increasingly joined in partnership with other streams and denominations in Christian witness and in enabling the voice of Pentecostal believers to be heard on the important issues of our time. Elim have been committed members of the Evangelical Alliance (EA) for many years. In 2014 John Glass was elected Chair of the Evangelical Alliance Council, the first Pentecostal to hold such office in the EA's history. Secure in our own identity and doctrine we thank God for the opportunities we have to partner with brothers and sisters from other streams to see His kingdom come.

A fresh Elim logo for the Millennium was launched in partnership with Elim New Zealand and provided a strong sense of identity for Elim in the 2000s.

"The history of the world-wide Church in the 20th century is dominated by an amazing move of God with hundreds of millions coming to Christ, millions of Churches planted and the emergence of a fresh, radical and passionate expression of the Christian faith. From humble beginnings 100 years ago, Elim as part of this Pentecostal movement, has profoundly influenced the Church here in the UK.

I, and millions like me, have benefited from a fresh discovery of the work of the Holy Spirit, both in individual lives and in the body of Christ.

I'm thankful that Elim is not resting on its history but is looking forward to playing its part in the purposes of God in our generation.

Steve Clifford, General Director, Evangelical Alliance

evangelical alliance
better together

SECTION 2
Embracing Our Future

DNA
diːɛnˈeɪ/

the fundamental and distinctive characteristics or qualities of someone or something, especially when regarded as unchangeable.

Elim's DNA consists of those priorities and commitments that we consider God given non-negotiables of spiritual heritage and destiny that must shape and define us in the next century …

A baptism in the sea at Perranporth, Cornwall,
where a new Elim church with a difference has been opened.

CHURCH PLANTING

Elim is committed to planting and pioneering new churches and to re-purposing and renewing existing churches. We are dedicated to releasing our resources and giftings and to mobilising a rising generation to see life-giving church communities established in every city, town and village in the nation. We believe that the church expresses its true purpose when it is moving forward in mission. We do not seek to depend simply on models and formulas but to develop a dependence on the power and ministry of the Holy Spirit.

A New Way of Doing Church

New Wave Church, Perranporth

Matt Timms had been assistant minister at a thriving Elim church for nine years when he and his wife Sally sensed God leading them to give it all up to go and plant a new Christian community in the midst of the surfing community of north Cornwall.

Rather than immediately opening a Sunday service, they began by investing time and energy in being with unchurched people whether on the beach or in homes.

"To some people this may sound fairly chaotic," says Matt. "But we're trying to reach a culture that's very transient, nomadic and highly relational."

Matt and Sally began praying for a "person of peace" (Luke 9) who would be a catalyst to get things going. A connection happened with a couple who had been totally de-churched for ten years. What began there with Sunday afternoon food and Bible study has become the foundation of New Wave Church.

They still feed everyone at Sunday lunch – sometimes it's fifty adults and forty children! As the church pastor, he is keen to stay away from his desk as much as possible to be where people are, being "a friend of sinners" and seeking to help people become Jesus' followers.

NEW WAVE CHURCH
WWW.NEWWAVECHURCH.CO.UK

> **"** If you try to build the church, you will rarely get disciples; but if you make disciples, you will always get the church.
>
> One of Matt's favourite quotes by Mike Breen.

Church with a difference - reaching o
to the surfer community in Perranporth, Cornwa

Corby

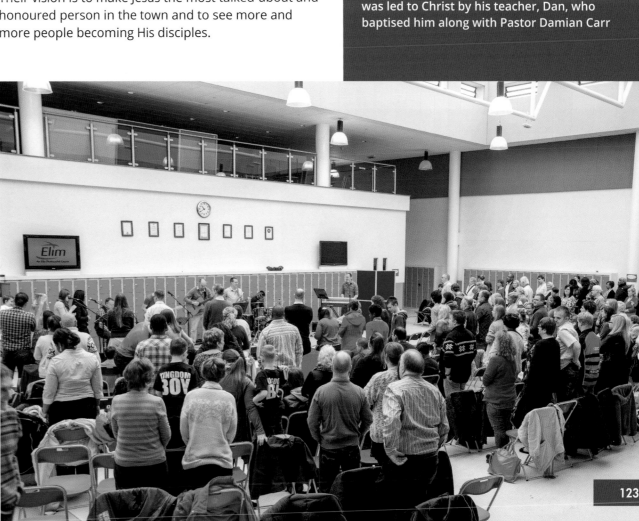

In 1994 as a newly saved follower of Jesus, Damian Carr stood one evening with his church house group at the end of a newly built road which came to an abrupt end, blocked by a big mound of mud. They prayed for those who would come to live on a yet-to-be-built housing estate in the town of Corby. They asked for God to build His church in that place. At that moment, Damian had a sense that, somehow, he would be part of the answer to that prayer.

Fast forward to 2008. Damian, now an Elim minister, returned with his family and began to pray with a small group of people who became the founding members of Hope Church, Corby.

The church launched publicly on November 16 that year in a primary school on the very estate which Damian had prayed for 14 years earlier. They were astounded at the number of people who came to the launch service. It felt as though God's favour was very much on the ministry.

In less than two years, they had outgrown the primary school. In 2014, after continued growth, Hope Church (West) was launched on the other side of town. This would mean, in effect, that they became "one church in two locations".

Over the six years since Hope Church opened, they have seen numerous salvations and Christians growing in faith and maturity. Their purpose statement as a church expresses their passion to put Jesus at the centre of it all, *"We want to see people moving towards Jesus: ourselves (maturity); our church (ministry) and our world (mission)".*

Their vision is to make Jesus the most talked-about and honoured person in the town and to see more and more people becoming His disciples.

One of the first converts at Corby and the church's first outdoor baptism; Arran France was led to Christ by his teacher, Dan, who baptised him along with Pastor Damian Carr

Ignite Church, Lincoln

***D**arren Edwards leads Ignite Church on a large housing estate in Lincoln. Saved in Northampton from a life of drugs and criminality, Darren is a great example of how God rescues and restores individuals. Here he tells the story of the church.*

The Vision

In 2009, whilst serving a community in Northampton I felt the need to bring a relevant, Spirit-filled church to the estate where we were working. This desire birthed a vision to plant a similar church on other

Connecting with youngsters on the local estate.

estates. I felt an impression from heaven that Lincoln should be the first of these.

In 2010 I attended Regents Theological College with the aim of being equipped to carry out the vision. During my time there I learnt about the concept of "organic church" – letting the people from the community build the culture of a church. I also learnt about Evan Roberts and George Jeffreys, and how their ministries attracted ordinary people.

My vision soon became one of emulating the ministry of these two revivalists by raising up a working class church within a working class community.

Our Church

In 2013 we hit the floor running after years of refining the vision and months of planning. On September 1, 2013, we had our first service, and ten to fifteen people joined us from the community. By September 1, 2014, we had a core of around twenty Christians, and another thirty to forty people who attend our church regularly.

We have seen agoraphobics filled with the Spirit of God and begin to go shopping by themselves. We have seen people filled with God's Spirit from the age of eleven to

A new convert is baptised

seventy-eight. We have seen God heal a diabetic ulcer on someone's toe, and all sorts of other physical healings – from back problems to a young boy's broken body, after being hit by a van.

In 2015 we'll start our first internship to raise up new leaders and church planters from among our own and further abroad.

Church Planting

As the centenary of the movement approached churches were asked to seriously consider planting a new work. Called "The Big Centenary Ask", the challenge was to plant a daughter church, another campus or a "fresh expression" of church. Elim now has more active plants happening than at any time in its history. Three examples are highlighted in these pages, but there are many more we could have shown. This will continue as a major area of investment and growth as we seek to re-evangelise areas of "darkest Britain".

Pioneering and planting churches is part of Elim's heritage and is how the movement was birthed. Typically, George Jeffreys and his Elim "Revival Party" would begin a series of meetings, often in a marquee or a hall. Early on, a significant healing would take place as a result of prayer. Within a short space of time the meetings would move to a much larger auditorium as news of the dramatic healing would spread. The meetings would usually continue for several weeks until the Revival Party moved on and a pioneer pastor would follow up on those who had made decisions to follow Christ.

A Sunday service would start and a new church was born. This method proved remarkably successful for over thirty years as Elim's primary means of church planting.

Elim's *modus operandi* for church planting remained largely unchanged throughout the 20th Century.

Ministries such as P.S. Brewster, Alex Tee, Wynne Lewis, Paul Epton and others were used by God to begin new Christian communities.

Once planted, each Elim church retained a strong evangelistic emphasis. In particular, the Sunday evening service was given over to Gospel proclamation. Elim worked hard at remaining as contemporary as possible in its style of worship music as the decades moved along.

This, combined with clear salvation testimonies, fervent preaching of God's Good News and a willingness by church members to invite people to the services resulted in much salvation growth. In this fresh season we are excited to see a new wave of church planting through a huge variety of means and methods.

EVANGELISM

Evangelism is at the heart of the Elim Movement. Sharing the Good News of the gospel in relevant and accessible ways remains our priority. Our Constitution states that we exist to "...spread and propagate the full Gospel of our Lord Jesus Christ..."

In recent years, many Elim churches have repurposed themselves for mission both through fresh initiatives to serve and reach out to the surrounding communities and by planting new Christian communities in places where there is little viable Gospel witness. The creativity, energy and supernatural enabling for all of this takes us back to the roots from when Elim began.

REACH - Evangelizing in the 21ˢᵗ Century

REACH
turning inside out

Partnering with Elim Churches, taking God's good news into communities in culturally relevant ways

EVANGELISM + CHURCH PLANTING

REACH is Elim's National Evangelism and Church Planting Department
Registered Charity 251549 (England & Wales) SC037754 (Scotland)

Elim

As the national evangelism and church planting department of Elim, REACH is a catalyst and facilitator for a missional movement within Elim, equipping and empowering the local church for effective evangelism ministry and church planting, in order to see more people becoming effective disciples.

The Local Church - Transforming Communities

Realising that the world we live in has changed, but with the same historic spiritual DNA in place, Elim has adopted fresh approaches in order to reach people who are far away from God. In the local church, this has been exhibited in a number of ways, for example:

▶ The provision of ministries to meet felt needs such as debt counselling, food banks, parents and tots groups, senior citizens lunches, twelve step recovery groups, outreaches to the homeless.

▶ Power evangelism ministries through 'Healing on the Streets' teams, healing rooms, 'treasure hunting', healing services.

▶ Seeker sensitive or seeker aware services.

▶ Evangelism courses. Many churches have used courses such as Alpha and Christianity Explored with positive results.

DEFINING MOMENTS

Raising and Releasing Evangelists

We recognise the calling and ministry of evangelists and see these women and men as gifts to our movement.

Historically and still today there are a small number of travelling evangelists who work alongside our churches to both *'equip God's people for works of service'* (Ephesians 4:12) and to powerfully preach the Gospel in a variety of contexts, often with signs, wonders and miracles following. In the future, we hope that as well as these ministries we will experience a rise in the number of local church-based evangelists who will work with the other local leaders to maintain and foster an outward culture and practice.

A popular saying at this time is that "the best is yet to come!" There is generally within Elim an optimism – or rather, a faith – that even in the midst of a western culture which seems to have drifted far from its Judaeo-Christian roots, every one of us now has the opportunity to be missionaries in our own land.

> " The harvest is still plentiful; there are lost people everywhere! God looks to us to be workers in the harvest fields. To be a member of the Elim Movement and family is to be committed to this great task!
>
> Gary Gibbs, Director of REACH

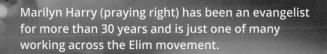

Marilyn Harry (praying right) has been an evangelist for more than 30 years and is just one of many working across the Elim movement.

TRAINING

E lim Training is committed to supporting and strengthening the local church. Our vision is to see everyone serving within Elim anointed and equipped to serve God into this century. We have a passion for developing authentic and resilient leaders and for enabling them to navigate the changing landscape. To achieve this, Elim training draws on experienced and seasoned leaders and those gifted in specific ministries to fashion and shape training resources that are relevant, dynamic and accessible. With the world class facilities and resources of Regents Theological College, we have a centre of excellence for ministry training. Alongside this we celebrate and encourage lifelong leadership development and the impact of "iron sharpening iron" mentoring and coaching. Our training mandate rests upon our conviction that this Elim generation can believe and trust God to fill them with His Holy Spirit for the adventure of ministry into our second century.

Elim Training Priorities

Knowing
By learning about God, self and the world

Being
By personal relationship with God

Doing
By living a life of service

Elim Training
Leadership | Study Opportunities | Resources | elim.org.uk/training

Elim training places a priority on three important areas:

Knowledge

The importance of growing in knowledge – of the Bible, our faith, and our practices – relating to our head/thinking.

Character

The importance of loving God more and allowing our love for Him to transform who we are. Creating excellent spiritual disciplines relating to our heart and character.

Action

The importance of living out of "what we know" and "who we are". We believe great training affects what we do. We are compelled to mission and discipleship.

Regents Theological College

Regents Theological College (RTC) is Elim's Bible College where people, passionate about Jesus, grow in their knowledge, skills and enthusiasm for serving God. For 90 years we have been preparing people from all walks of life for world-impacting Christian service in a variety of Christian and secular contexts. Our exciting and comprehensive range of training opportunities include a programme that can be tailored to all needs.

In partnership with the University of Chester, RTC offers a year School of Ministry, three year full time programmes (or part-time over six years) and four Masters degree programmes (one year full-time; two to three years part-time). Graduates from RTC serve in church and ministry situations all over the world.

▶ Intentional learning

▶ Intentional transformation

▶ Intentional service

Training for the Real World

Elim has approximately fifty Chaplains working in areas including education, healthcare, prisons, the armed forces and the emergency services. Elim Training brings together Chaplains, so that they can get to know others working in similar fields, and to share knowledge and best practice.

WORD&SPIRIT

Word & Spirit is dedicated to engagements with the Bible and encounters with God in ways that are accessible, enjoyable and life-transforming. *Word & Spirit* has one main objective – to enable leaders and other believers to engage efficiently and enthusiastically with the Bible in ways that reflect our belief that it is a collection of God's words to us.

7. Uzbekistan

9. Iraq

5. Iran

2. Afghanistan

10. Pakistan

3. Saudi Arabia

8. Yemen

4. Somalia

6. Maldives

MISSIONS

Birthed in the wake of a spirit of evangelism and church planting, Elim International Missions are involved in nearly fifty countries around the world, sending missionaries to many different situations, but all with the same aim of reaching people with the good news of Jesus Christ.

The story of Elim is left untold without telling of the influence the movement has had, and continues to have, in the farthest parts of the world. Countless adventures continue to unfold as Elim people respond to God's call to the nations with radical obedience and faith.

Nearly a hundred years on, the same three components found on opening day of Elim Missions are still calling for engagement today: a church, a missionary and the Holy Spirit. Elim Missions is still here to stand with a sending church, to support the empowered missionary and to listen to and follow the Spirit. This is why we exist. This is still the prayerful call of Elim International Missions, to follow the example of those who have gone before us and to surrender ourselves to the Lord of the Harvest by praying, giving and going to the people of other nations.

Elim Missions Around the World

In 1919, only four years after the founding of the Elim Pentecostal Church, Elim's pioneer leaders sent their first missionary overseas. During the season of Elim becoming a movement known for planting churches, miraculous healings and powerful evangelistic events, one lady, Dollie Phillips, went with a steely determination and raw passion to take the gospel to those who had never heard the Gospel as she sailed for Mumbai, India. Others, like Cyril Taylor and Adelaide Henderson, also responded to the call to the nations in those first few years, but it would be a decade until a more intentional overseas missions ministry was established. Originally called The Elim Missionary Society this was founded in 1929. The Second World War curtailed missionary expansion, but in 1945 and over following decades Elim missionaries went out to many countries in Africa, South America and Asia.

Dollie Phillips, the first Elim missionary who went to Mumbai, India, in 1919.

"In order to reach the tribe from the po of Rio de Janeiro, a journey of nearly two months is involved. Approximately six days by rail, seven or more days b steam-boat, twenty by mule, twelve by canoe, with five or more days to build canoes, and more days (or perhaps weeks) waiting for connections. The journey is over mountains, plains, rivers, and across stretches of country that few, if any, white men have ever trodden. At times rivers must be forded bridges built, paths made.

Harold H. Cook, missionary in Brazil, describing his journ to the Xingu Indians about two thousand miles from the coast of Brazil in the Elim Evangel, 1929.

The Elim work in India in the 1980s

H. C. Phillips, brother of Dollie, baptising a new convert in Africa, where he served for many years.

Our Vision – Our Passion

Church Planting

Part of the vision of Elim Missions is to stand with the sending church and that means not only doing good work around the world but doing it through the local church. Without local church we cannot do all we are called to do.

Human Exploitation

Be Free is Elim Missions' campaign against human exploitation. There are between 2-4 million people trafficked across borders each year, 300,000 child soldiers working around the world and approximately 3,287 men, women and children being taken and sold every day. We are currently working in Cambodia, DRC, India and Indonesia where we have missionaries and partner organisations working to help and rehabilitate those who are victims of human exploitation.

Persecuted Church

Working alongside our partners, church and missionaries, Elim Missions is committed to standing alongside the persecuted church.

According to the Pew Research Centre, Christians face harassment and intimidation in 145 countries worldwide. In a number of countries where they constitute a religious minority, this treatment can range from discrimination, harassment, and violence by state and non-state actors, to imprisonment or death.

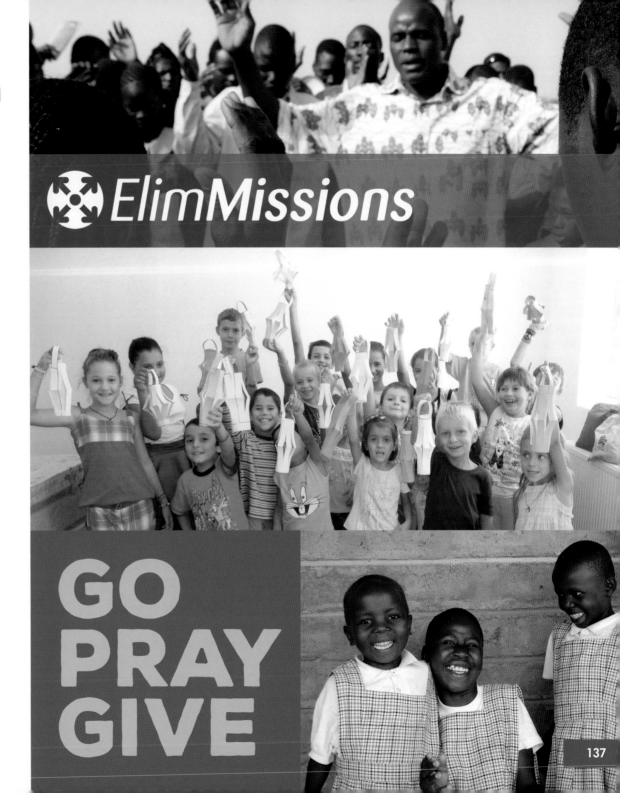

Taking the Message of Jesus Christ to the Nations

CENTRAL & SOUTHERN AFRICA

PAUL & TRACY GILL
MALAWI

CLAIR OATES
SWAZILAND

GORDON & SYBIL MCKILLOP
ZAMBIA

ZISO & NICKI MOYO
ZAMBIA

JANE BRADSHAW
SWAZILAND

LLOYD & JOANNE CHESHIRE
SWAZILAND

WENDY BROWN
SWAZILAND

JACKIE GRIFFITHS
MALAWI

FARAI KATIRO
ZIMBABWE

TREVOR & MAGGIE MACKRIELL
MALAWI

GEOFF & ERICKA SAUNDERS
ZIMBABWE

ROBIN & JANET FENNER
SOUTH AFRICA

ASIA

BECKY HALDANE
INDONESIA

NOVI & SHERYL MAATITAWAER
INDONESIA

NIGEL & RACHEL STUDLEY
INDIA

REUBEN & TAMARA
MIDDLE EAST

ANDREW & LAURA BLEAKLEY
NEPAL

ANDREW & KATHRYN
MIDDLE EAST

LYNETTE ORANGE
PHILIPPINES

BHAB GHALE
NEPAL

Elim International Missions was birthed in the wake of a spirit of evangelism and church planting. Nearly 100 years after the first early pioneers went overseas Elim now has missionaries working in around 50 countries world-wide. Paul Hudson is the current International Missions Director.

DAVID & ESTHER ALLEN
CAMBODIA

DEFINING MOMENTS

EAST & WEST AFRICA

KIPPY & PAUL AGYEI
SIERRA LEONE

TIM & ALI ROBINSON
NIGERIA

SIAN DAVIES
UGANDA

BOUREIMA & SUSANNA DIALLO
BURKINA FASO

TERRY & JUDI MOTT
ZAMBIA

IAN & HILDA MCMILLAN
KENYA

SHAUN & KAREN GRAHAM
TANZANIA

EUROPE

MARTIN & RUTH MOHR
FRANCE

TONY & NORMA COLES
MACEDONIA

HOWARD & SUE COLEY
SPAIN

JAMES & MARIA
LONDON

PHIL & ANNEKE TAYLOR
SWEDEN

RICH & REGI ELLERINGTON
FRANCE

DANIEL & DAWN DAWKINS
ITALY

ROY & ELAINE HITCHMAN
HUNGARY

JOHN & VALERIE KNOX
SPAIN

DAVID & NAOMI HODGSON
SPAIN

BOB & EDITH MCDONALD
ROMANIA

ALI & FRANCOISE ARHAB
FRANCE

CRISTIAN & BECKY TUDOSIE
ROMANIA

LIZ FACE
ROMANIA

THE AMERICAS

MARTIN & REBECA DAVISON
BRAZIL

JOHN & RACHEL MCDONOUGH
PARAGUAY

Elim Global

> Elim is a global
> movement of local
> churches, authentic
> locally, acting globally.
>
> Mark Ryan

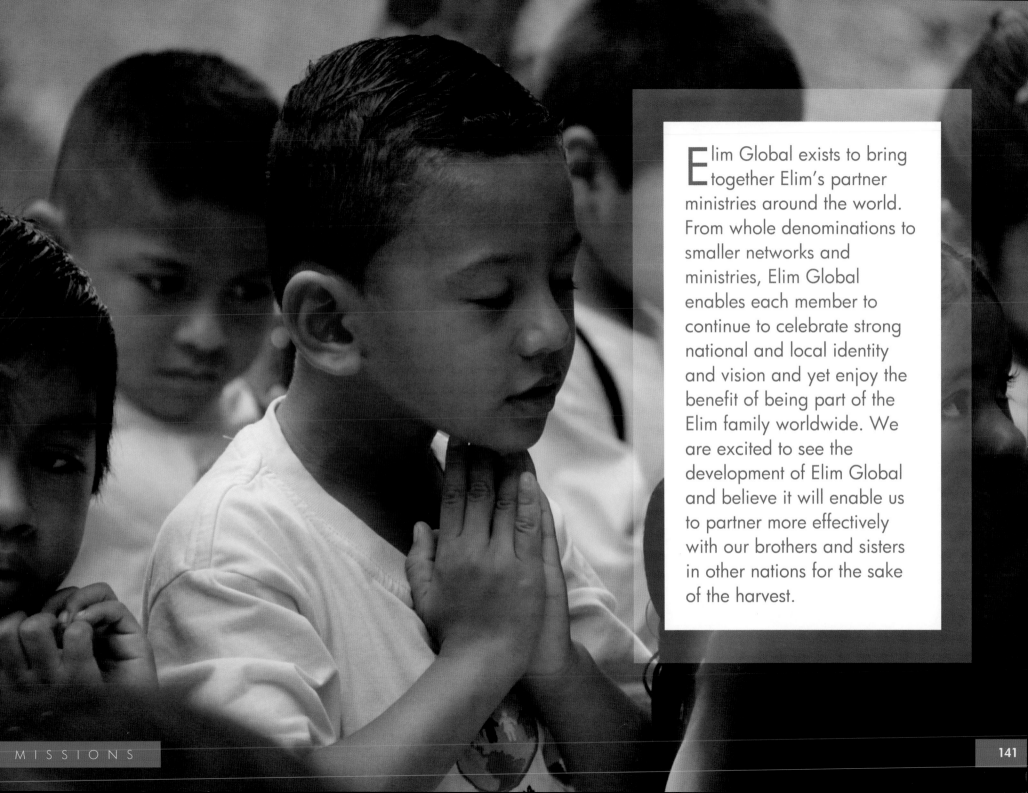

Elim Global exists to bring together Elim's partner ministries around the world. From whole denominations to smaller networks and ministries, Elim Global enables each member to continue to celebrate strong national and local identity and vision and yet enjoy the benefit of being part of the Elim family worldwide. We are excited to see the development of Elim Global and believe it will enable us to partner more effectively with our brothers and sisters in other nations for the sake of the harvest.

YOUTH

At Serious4God we passionately believe in young people. There is no background or life experience that disqualifies young people from living out the potential that God has placed within them – the potential to be changers of other people's worlds.

Serious4God is the national youth ministry of the Elim churches in UK and Ireland. We exist to do three things:

- **REACH YOUNG PEOPLE FOR CHRIST**

- **EQUIP YOUTH LEADERS** and

- **INSPIRE DYNAMIC YOUTH MINISTRY THROUGH THE LOCAL CHURCH**

It is a stirring ministry that is not content with settling, but is inspired to see young people rise up in God and prove to society that the Jesus they worship is very much alive and powerfully at work.

The Gathering

Serious4God brings young people from across the Elim movement together once a year for a massive celebration called *The Gathering*. Over the years *The Gathering* has proved to be a major highlight in the Elim calendar, as churches and youth groups unite for a powerful weekend of dynamic worship, inspirational teaching and incredible atmosphere. In October 2007, *The Gathering Max* took place at the National Exhibition Centre, Birmingham. This incredible event saw more than 1000 people saved in a single day!

Serious4God Ministries

At *Serious4God* we are committed to training up the next generation of youth leaders. Our *Rise Up* programme at Regents Theological College combines exciting weekly placements, youth ministry training, theological study and discipleship formation, to nurture bold and courageous leaders who will impact a generation which so desperately needs Jesus.

We believe that the local church is the hope of the world. This is as true for the younger generations as it is for anyone. The Elim movement, through *Serious4God*, is committed to cutting edge ministry that will relevantly engage with our evolving culture, challenging secularism with an everlasting truth: that Jesus Christ is God *'yesterday, today and forever'*. Our method will constantly change, our mission will remain resolutely the same. We will not let a generation pass by who do not hear the gospel proclaimed. We trust you will join us.

To find out more about *Serious4God* visit:
www.serious4god.co.uk

WORSHIP

More than simply lively meetings and enthusiastic singing, the Elim movement has been characterised by gatherings in which music and corporate worship is a vital part of the Holy Spirit's work. From mission halls to tent meetings and campaign meetings in the largest halls in the nation, the emerging Elim movement and people experienced in vibrant and heartfelt worship the tangible and manifest presence of God. Elim today continues to encourage every believer to live with an experience of the presence and power of God through a lifestyle of personal and corporate worship. It is our desire to seek to release the full gifting and creativity that God has given through song, music and the wider palette of creative arts to the glory of God.

Elim Sound -
A Worship Movement

Elim Sound, founded in 2010 by Sam Blake, Stephen Gibson, Joel Pridmore and Ian Yates, is Elim's national worship ministry. It was birthed out of a desire to equip the church with the skills and attitudes which can build strong worshipping churches. Assisted by area coordinators, *Elim Sound* team is developing training opportunities to inspire the church to worship, equip worship leaders and musicians and encourage creativity. The *School of Worship*, launched in 2013, seeks to influence those in worship ministry in their local church to help them develop and grow in their gifting. The School provides opportunity for worship leaders, singers and musicians to experience excellent musical and biblical teaching that will ultimately impact their church.

Elim Sound have a rich heritage that spans almost an entire century and are the product of a new generation emerging within the UK's Elim Pentecostal churches. Bringing together a community of worship leaders, pastors and creative people from the Elim movement and beyond, *Elim Sound* are committed to inspiring, encouraging and equipping the church in worship.

Passion for Worship

Elim is blessed with a huge range of musical gifting and ministry within its churches. Many national and international worship leaders and ministries are connected with Elim. Together they recognise the growing challenge and opportunity to release and encourage a new generation to believe and work together for a fresh and powerful overflow of praise and worship. It is our desire to seek to release the full gifting and creativity that God has given through song, music and the wider palette of creative arts to the glory of God.

PRAYER

As Elim stands on the threshold of another century, prayer and mission are the key ingredients of spiritual renewal both in terms of the church and the nation. God is mobilising the most powerful prayer army in the history of the Christian church. Elim is very much part of this great move of God as we look to the future.

The early Elim pioneers were a generation that were imbued with a passion to reach people for Christ. Major towns and cities the length and breadth of the nation were impacted as the gospel was preached in the power and dynamic of the Holy Spirit. Their power to preach, and demonstrate the gospel of the Kingdom, was built upon a foundation of prevailing prayer. Men and women cried to God in prayer, often around the clock, for the salvation of the lost. Prayer became a key factor in the establishing of vibrant centres of Pentecostal witness.

Elim's prayer ministry seeks to encourage every individual and every church to commit to a lifestyle of prayer. Our mission and outreach continue to be fuelled by faith filled prayer and confidence that God answers prayer.

"Pray Without Ceasing"

Elim's Centenary celebrations will not be just an exercise in mere nostalgia. This milestone year should serve not only to reflect upon our history, but also to forge ahead in terms of renewed mission and vision. In preparation for the anniversary an initiative, LIFT UP 2014, called churches and individuals to make the year leading up to the Centenary one of special prayer.

As Elim churches respond to The Big Centenary Ask they are following in the footsteps of the early Pentecostal pioneers who sought to establish centres of witness in our towns and cities. Missional activity such as this is the very DNA of our Elim movement. The success of this venture will be determined by the level of prayer undertaken. The theme LIFT UP is taken from Psalm 121, sung by Jewish pilgrims to celebrate the great Jewish Feasts. In the same we called our Elim churches to pray to see breakthrough and transformation in our families, our communities, our nation and beyond in this Centenary year.

I lift up my eyes to the mountains – where does my help come from? My help comes from the LORD, the Maker of heaven and earth.

Psalm 121:1,2

"My help comes from the LORD..."

FASTING 2014

REDISCOVERING JESUS...

January 9th-30th

"... a little child will lead them..." Isaiah 11:6

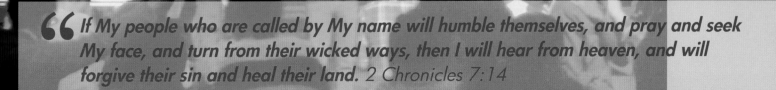

> *If My people who are called by My name will humble themselves, and pray and seek My face, and turn from their wicked ways, then I will hear from heaven, and will forgive their sin and heal their land.* 2 Chronicles 7:14

CHAPTER TWENTY–ONE

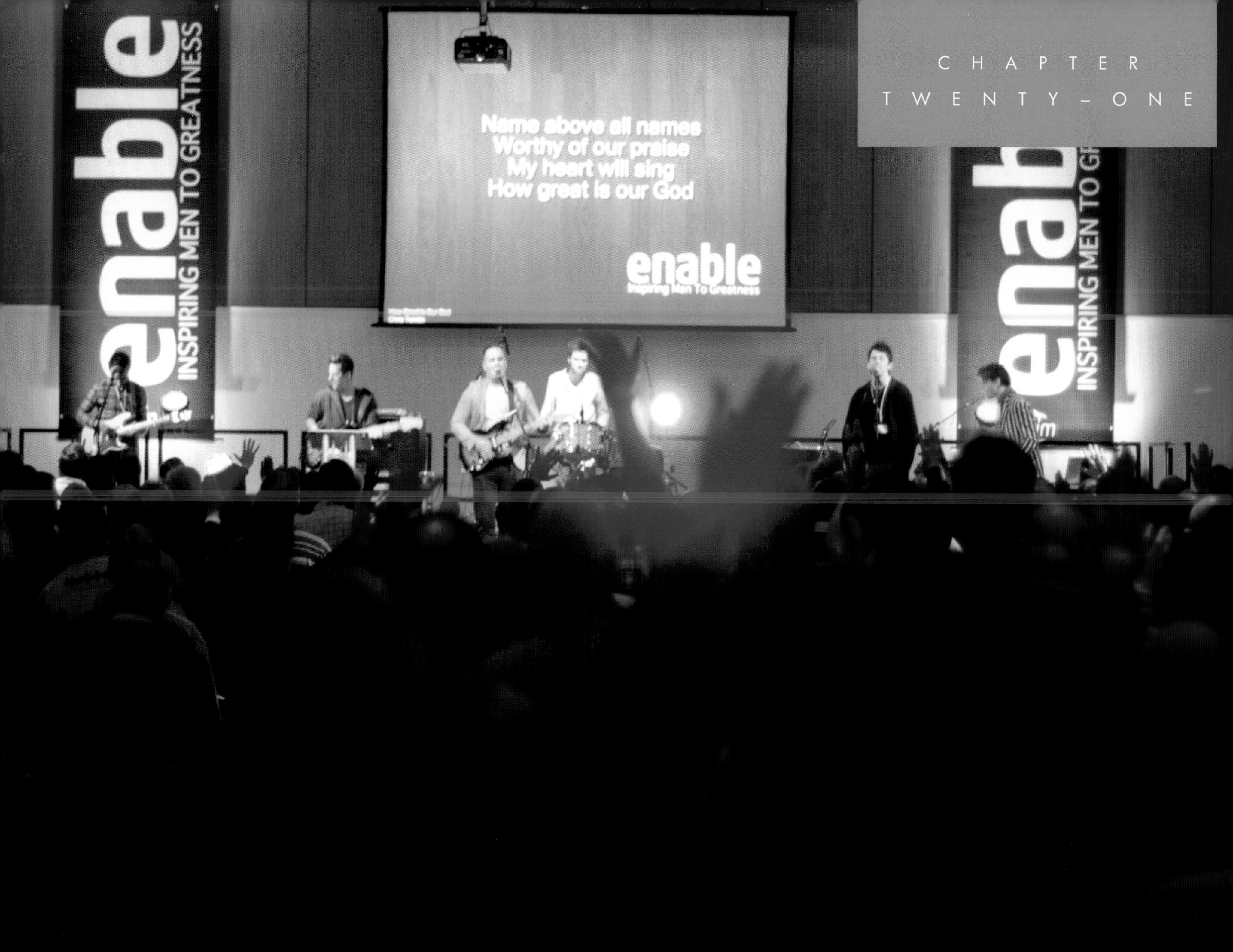

MPOWER MEN'S MINISTRY

As we "Honour the Past" and "Embrace the Future" the goal of MPOWER, Elim's National Men's Ministry, is to build a spiritual heritage for the rising generations of men within our movement.

Living the Christian life in contemporary society stretches and tests guys on many levels, ranging from financial management to resisting the technological temptations of internet pornography as well as balancing work, life, family and church. MPOWER is calling out spiritual fathers and sons in our movement to engage in some "Iron Sharpening" that will hone their God given character and qualities, addressing today's issues to shape tomorrow's outcomes.

Our world is crying out for effective male role models both socially and spiritually, and MPOWER has the opportunity to raise up generations of men in authentic, nation-shaping Christianity.

Engaging guys to do "life together" as brothers in Christ will benefit their families, churches and communities through a growing confidence in Christ which MPOWER will offer through mutual encouragement, equipping and resourcing as Elim's National Men's Ministry – building a future spiritual heritage today.

Raising a New Generation of Men

*E*ngaging men of all ages, by exploring the potential to mentor a generation of radical disciples. The result? Men – resourced and equipped to impact the future. Addressing the unique challenges of manhood and masculinity, helping forge a plan and a purpose for future generations. MPOWER – encouraging the masculine journey into true wholeness for the future.

Gathering at an Elim men's conference

Being an 'authentic man in Christ'

MPOWER is the process whereby one generation empowers the rising generations of sons, brothers and fathers in our movement to be authentic men in Christ, in life and in church.

MPOWER

EMPOWERING
AUTHENTIC
MEN

ELIM'S NATIONAL MEN'S MINISTRY

ASPIRE WOMEN'S MINISTRY

Aspire is Elim's National Women's Ministry. It was birthed in 2007 and is the first national women's ministry in the 100 year history of Elim. It cares for and connects with women to encourage them to be all that God has called them to be and to equip them to fulfil His purposes.

Caring for Women

*A*spire is run by a committed National team as well as regional coordinators who are passionate about serving God and supporting His women of influence within our movement.

Our Aims

Aspire organises conferences and connects with local churches who are linked to Aspire to give encouragement and advice. Each month *Direction*, Elim's national magazine, includes an Aspire page to inspire women and keep them updated with Aspire events.

DEFINING MOMENTS

Passionate for God

Our Values

- Ambitious to make a difference in women's lives
- Selfless in serving God's leading ladies
- Passionate about God
- Influential in all the right places
- Resourceful in all that we provide
- Excellent in all that we present

ONE CHURCH
MANY CHURCHES

WORSHIPPING GOD | MAKING DISCIPLES

SERVING COMMUNITIES | REACHING PEOPLE

ONE CHURCH
MANY CHURCHES

DEFINING MOMENTS

ELIMLIFE
CHURCH KINGSTANDING

OFFICES
COMMUNITY HALL
LIFE CAFÉ
FOODBANK

0121 350 9650 | www.elimlifechurch.co.uk

EDINBURGH
elimchurch Welcome!
AN ELIM PENTECOSTAL CHURCH

Sundays at 11am and 6pm
www.edinburghelim.com

ONE CHURCH
MANY CHURCHES

DEFINING MOMENTS

Jesus Christ the same Yesterday and Today and Forever

Elim
An oasis in the desert

Monaghan Elim Church
The Birthplace of the Elim Movement

Sharing Jesus' love
spreading his message
Telling his story

ONE CHURCH
MANY CHURCHES

DEFINING MOMENTS

CONFIDENT

We are confident. Not brash, egotistical, arrogant or proud.
Not pessimistic, cynical, despairing or 'glass half-empty' Christians.
We are confident.

Confident that the gospel message changes lives. Confident that the
Bible has authority for life today. Confident that Jesus still saves and
the Spirit empowers. Confident in God's ability to heal bodies and
transform communities. Confident that the church has a significant
future. Confident that Christ will return one day.
We are confident.

And so, we will pray bold prayers, dream big dreams, create
forward momentum and believe that through God we will prevail.
We will plant churches, reach communities, teach passionately and
love outrageously. We will not hold back.

We're not conceited or smug, we are confident.

Duncan Clark

THE CENTENARY NATIONAL LEADERSHIP TEAM

Back Row: Stuart Blount, Colin Dye, Dave Campbell, Mark Pugh, Duncan Clark, Simon Foster, Kevin Peat.
Front Row: James Glass, John Glass, Chris Cartwright, Gordon Neale.

POSITIONED FOR ANOTHER CENTURY

Elim's history is filled with moments which have shaped our destiny. We are believing for many such moments in the days and years to come. Encouraged and strengthened by the past, we look to embrace our future inspired by what God has already done but leaning into all that the Holy Spirit still longs to do through the Elim movement.

Chris Cartwright

> "Every human action gains in honour, in grace, in all true magnificence, by its regard to things that are to come...Therefore, when we build, let us think that we build forever. Let it not be for present delight, nor for present use alone; let it be such work as our descendants will thank us for, and let us think, as we lay stone on stone, that a time is to come when those stones will be held sacred because our hands have touched them, and that men will say as they look upon the labour and wrought substance of them, "See! This our fathers did for us.""

John Ruskin

> "I see a church that is living authentically in this world and making a difference, standing for justice, having impact in every sphere of life. Elim people, not confined to buildings, but out there in every community being salt and light."

Dominic DeSouza

> "Elim is a movement that has been tried and tested over a hundred years. It's old but it's new, it's vintage but it's contemporary, it's familiar but it's fresh. God is wanting to bring us back to our original design and to release again the significance of this movement in our nation.
>
> That involves every person fully involved with the Christ call on their life living the unique adventure that Jesus has for them."

Simon Foster

> "Since we are surrounded by so great a cloud of witnesses, let us throw off everything that hinders and the sin that so easily entangles. And let us run with perseverance the race marked out for us, fixing our eyes on Jesus, the pioneer and perfecter of our faith."

Hebrews 12:1-2

> "We normally think of history as one catastrophe after another...But history is also the narratives of grace, the recounting of those blessed and inexplicable moments when someone did something for someone else, saved a life, bestowed a gift, gave something beyond what was required by circumstance."

Thomas Cahill

> "If so much was achieved from the days when George Jeffreys started out with a lowly half-dozen, what will the future produce, starting now with Elim's extensive resources – and the same Holy Spirit?"

George Canty, writing in 1983

> "As we minister in the early years of the 21st century we should be looking forward, rather than backward. But to prepare for this, we must first return to the fervour of primitive, pioneer Pentecostalism. We must seek God for a restoration of a full-blooded and radical Pentecostalism. This will include a revival of all the gifts of the Spirit both within our churches and out in the marketplace."

Bruce Atkinson

It's our time!

CONTACT US

ELIM INTERNATIONAL CENTRE
De Walden Road
West Malvern
Worcestershire UK
WR14 4DF
Tel: 0345 302 6750
Email: info@elimhq.net
www.elim.org.uk

REGENTS THEOLOGICAL COLLEGE
West Malvern Road
West Malvern
Worcestershire UK
WR14 4AY
Tel: 0345 302 6758
Email: info@regents-tc.ac.uk
www.regents-tc.ac.uk

ELIM CORPORATE OFFICES
14 Charlestown Avenue
Portadown
Co. Armagh UK
BT63 5ZF
Tel: 028 3833 5511
Email: info@elimchurchireland.com
www.elimireland.org

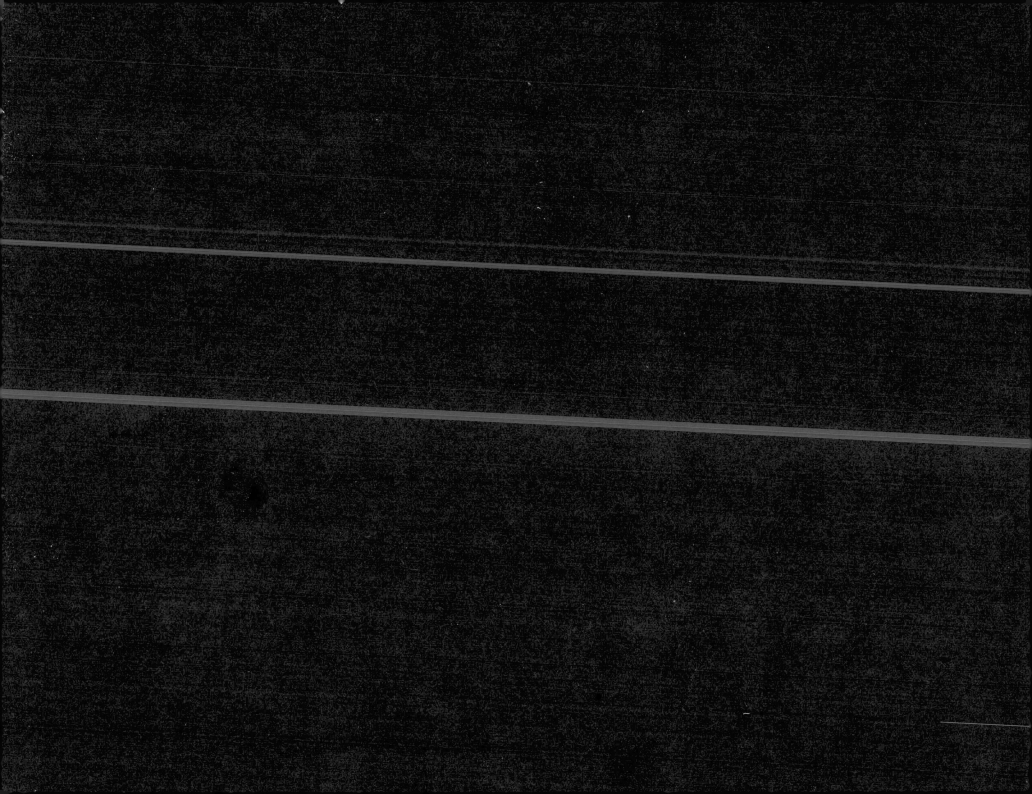